LIVING WITH A
Rescued Cat

Claire
Horton-Bus

THE QUESTION OF GENDER
The 'he' pronoun is used throughout this book in favour of the rather impersonal 'it', but no gender bias is intended.

ACKNOWLEDGEMENTS

Thanks to Cats Protection's veterinary consultant, Lisa Morrow, DipAppChemBiol, BMLSC, DVM, MRCVS, for her help with Chapters Four and Six, and Cats Protection's Lecturer in Feline Behaviour and Welfare, Rachel Casey, BVMS, DipCABC, MRCVS, for her advice and comments, particularly relating to Chapters Three and Five.
Photo on page 4 by Paul Keevil.
Photographs on front and back cover, and pages 6-7, courtesy of Cats Protection.

DEDICATION
For Dodie, Tiggy (One and Two), Tabbie, Paddie, Suki, Lady, Nobbie, Schuey, Georgie, Winnie, Bonnie, Morris, Roxy, Sammy, and, of course, my daughter Katie.

Published by Ringpress Books Ltd,
a division of Interpet Publishing,
Vincent Lane, Dorking, Surrey, RH4 3YX, UK

Designed by Sarah Williams.

First Published 2006
© 2006 RINGPRESS BOOKS

ISBN10: 1-86054-254-9
ISBN13: 978-1-86054-254-1

Printed and bound in China

0 9 8 7 6 5 4 3 2 1

FOREWORD

by Helen Ralston
Chief Executive, Cats Protection

I hope the reason why you are reading this book is that you have decided to bring a cat needing a new home into your life. Many cats have lost their original homes through no fault of their own, so I am glad that you are considering one of the many hard-working rescue organisations as the source of your new pet.

Cats *do not* come in many different shapes and sizes – but they *do* have an extraordinary range of personalities. There are those who want nothing more than a quiet lap available for as many hours as possible; those who enjoy the company of active children; those who prefer to live mainly outdoors and control the amount of contact with people; and those who are versatile enough to amuse themselves while you are out working but then love to welcome you home and be with you.

There are those who are instantly gregarious and those who take a long time to get to trust people – one of the eight cats I have had from Cats Protection over the years took more than three years before she chose to come on to my lap – but it was so rewarding when she did!

At Cats Protection we rehome about 60,000 cats a year from our 260 volunteer-run Branches and 29 Adoption Centres across the UK, so we will use our wealth of experience to ensure you find the right cat for your particular lifestyle. In *Living With a Rescued Cat* we try to consolidate useful information to prepare you for what may be a relationship lasting 20 years.

Cats come into rescue organisations for a multiplicity of reasons – such as an elderly owner dying or moving into sheltered accommodation that does not permit pets, relationship break-ups, emigration, a move for job reasons into rented housing with lease restrictions, allergies in the family – none of them of the cat's making. Yet these cats are willing to learn to trust people again at their own pace and to give you many hours of enjoyment.

Think carefully about the obligation you are taking on. Be prepared for the challenges that may come. Look forward to the delights of a cat bringing companionship and play into your life.

Then contact our helpline to locate where Cats Protection is close to you – and go find that right cat for you!

CONTENTS

1 CHOOSING A RESCUED CAT 9

Why choose a rescued cat?; Self-assessment; Choosing a cat (What age?; Male or female?; Moggie or purebred?; In or out? Coat type); Where to go (The charities); The process of adoption; Meeting the cats; Final step.

2 GETTING READY 31

Indoors and outdoors safety; Welcoming touches (Garden retreat; Home sweet home; The pen den; Cat-flap); Shopping list (Bed; Bowls; Litter tray; Cat litter; Toys; Collar); Vet search; Choosing a name.

3 SETTLING IN 51

Journey home; Arriving home; Litter training (What to do with the scoop; Accidents); Meeting the family (People and puss; Child's play; Fellow felines; Canine chums; Other furries); First night; Step outside… (In a flap).

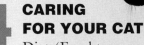

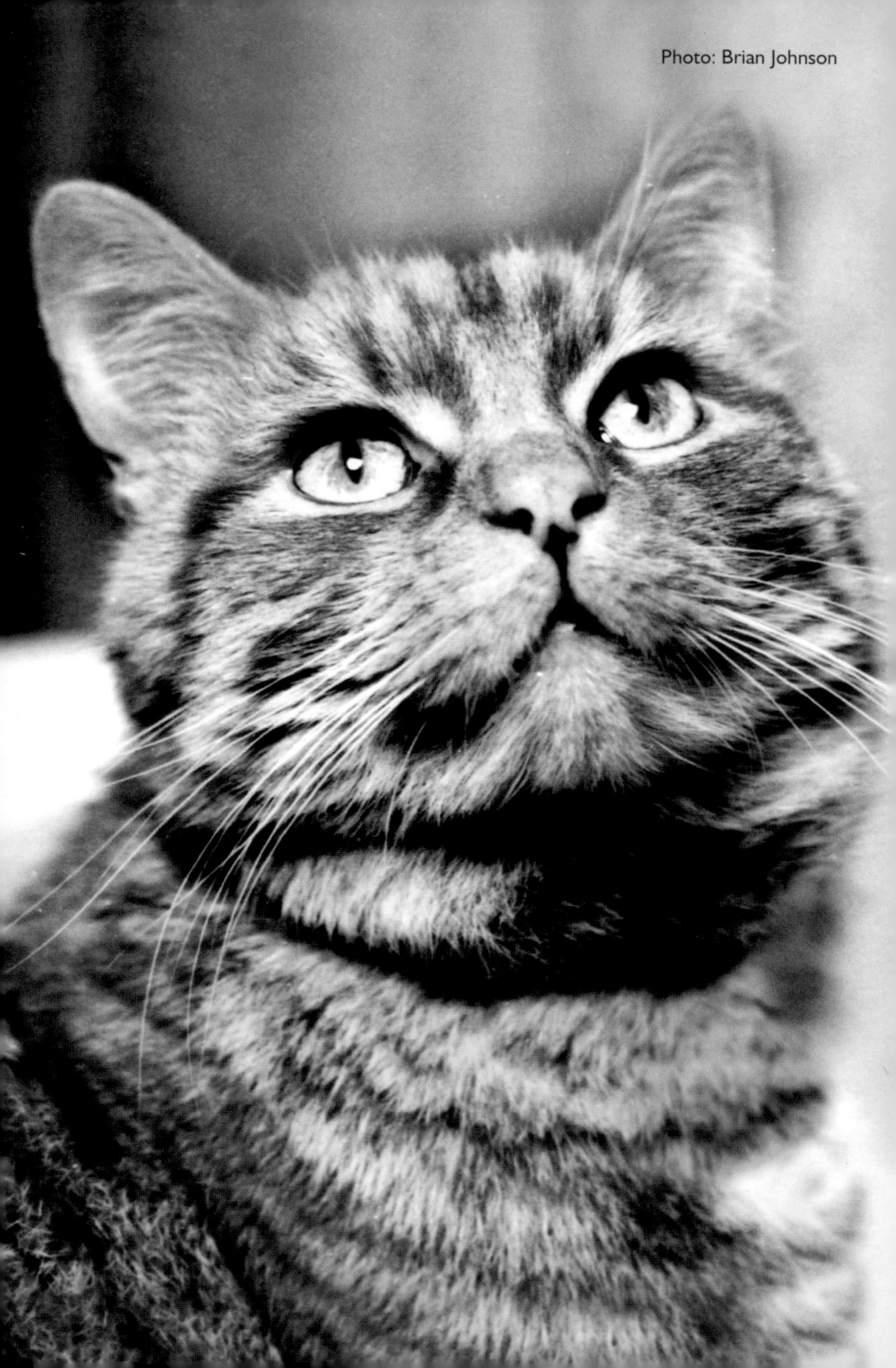
Photo: Brian Johnson

CHAPTER ONE

CHOOSING A RESCUED CAT

If you're reading this book, you are probably already aware that cats make fantastic pets. They are loving, warm, fun animals to share your life with, and they give so much pleasure and companionship to people from all walks of life. Whether young or old, a cat will give you his heart – if you can give him a lap!

Cats are relatively easy to care for – apart from basic preventative measures and everyday care, their main requirements are comfort and love. And with a cat's gorgeous good looks and irresistible character, it's very difficult NOT to crawl around on the living room floor with a catnip mouse, or spend an hour watching telly with a purring puss by your side.

With such fantastic qualities, it makes you wonder why there are any cats in rescue centres at all. There are a variety of reasons:

- Some are strays or have been abandoned.
- Some have become lost, and cannot be reunited with their owners, as there is no microchip or collar with identification.
- Some are unwanted kittens, where an unspayed pet female (queen) has produced a litter.
- Some are born feral (i.e. living wild) to a stray queen.

There are many different reasons why cats come into rescue centres.

Photo: Paul Keevil

- Some were much-loved pets that had to be rehomed because an elderly owner died or had to move into residential care where pets are not welcome.
- Some are given up if a family member develops an allergic reaction.
- Sadly, some are put up for rehoming because there's a new baby in the family (despite the fact that cats and kids can live happily and safely together – see page 60).
- Some are given up when their owners are moving abroad or to a place that is unsafe or unsuitable for a cat.
- Some come from multi-cat households where breeding has been allowed to take place, resulting in the owners no longer being able to cope, or the council ordering that the cats be rehomed.

So the reasons are numerous

and are rarely the fault of the cat, who just wants a stable, loving home and someone to cuddle up to.

WHY CHOOSE A RESCUED CAT?

The simple answer is: why not? There are lots of reasons why rehoming a rescued cat is preferable to buying a cat or kitten.

- Rescued cats from reputable organisations such as Cats Protection will have been assessed, to match them to the most suitable owners. Where information is available from the previous home, about a cat's experience of dogs, other cats and people, this will help ensure you have the right cat for your situation. Even if no information is available about the cat's former life, the staff will know his personality – whether he needs someone around a lot of the time or is content with someone who works, whether he likes other cats, and so on.

- Help will always be on the end of the phone. Most rescue centres offer advice free of charge if you are encountering difficulties. This is reassuring if, for example, your cat's behaviour changes – will you really be able to phone the person in the newspaper advert from five years ago?

- Why buy a kitten or cat when you can instead make a donation and adopt one that is homeless? There is a huge choice available – from youngsters to oldies, different coat colours and lengths, and different personalities. The only difficult decision will be choosing which one you want to take home!

- Some rescue cats may be a bit more challenging because of their previous bad experiences, but that just makes developing the relationship between you and your rescued cat even more rewarding.

Cats are very clever at making themselves feel at home – but weigh up the pros and cons before taking a cat into your family.

Photo: Richard Lovell

SELF-ASSESSMENT

Cats are versatile creatures. Provided their basic needs are catered for, and they are given sufficient opportunities for mental and physical stimulation, they can be as much at home in a flat as in a palace, although individual cats may differ in terms of the type of environment they are best suited to. Unlike dogs, they do not generally need an owner to be with them all the time, or to be taken out for two walks a day come rain or shine.

However, that's not to say that a cat is an 'easy' option – a part-time pet that needs no human interaction. A cat is not suitable for everyone. Rather than homing one on impulse, and him ending up in a rescue centre once more when it doesn't work out, it's important to be sure, from the start, that you can offer a responsible home.

Many rescue charities may ask to visit your home to carry out a 'matching' process, to ensure that the cat is likely to fit in with your circumstances and lifestyle.

- **Would a cat fit in with your family?** Realistically assess whether a cat is suitable in your family situation. In most cases having a cat with young children is very successful, but remember that the cat you choose should not be frightened of all the noise and excitement that occurs around children, and should not be left with young children without you being there to supervise – no animal should be expected to have wooden bricks rammed down his ears or be trampled by a toy scooter.

- **Your animal family should also be considered.** If you have a dog, is he cat-friendly? Dogs can be trained to accept cats, but you need to be prepared to spend the time training your dog in the short term, which may involve restricting him or her so that your new cat is not chased. If you already have cats, bringing a new cat into the home will be stressful for them. The naturally territorial nature of the cat means that unfamiliar cats in their area are seen as a big threat. You need to be prepared to follow a gradual programme of introduction to ensure that your existing cat(s) are stressed as little as possible by the arrival of the newcomer. If you have birds or rodents, is there a safe area where they can be kept, in a cat-free zone? It is important that these animals are not stressed by being in close proximity to your new cat, which is, of course, one of their natural predators.

- **Do you have the time for a cat?** The amount of time that a cat needs will vary with the individual cat. Some cats are of a more independent nature and may spend a lot of time out and about, and it may be sensible to consider a cat like this if you know you will be out of the house a lot of the time. Cats that are more dependent on people, and particularly those cats kept only indoors, will need much

Kittens are almost impossible to resist, but they are more labour intensive than adults.

Photo: Beverley Hill

more of your time and energy – both in the morning before work and when you come home in the evening. At weekends, he will need love too.

• **Are you very house-proud?** Cats are renowned for being clean creatures, but they can bring muddy footprints into the house if it's wet outside, they leave their hair on carpets and soft furnishings, long-haired cats particularly may occasionally cough up fur balls on your bed first thing in the morning, and some like to drop dead rodents in your slippers. If this would annoy you, choose another pet!

• **Is your local environment suitable for a cat?** The close proximity of a busy road can be a problem for cats that are not used to this, although often roads with intermittent traffic can be more of a problem. Risk of injury on a road can be reduced by constructing a safe, escape-proof outdoor pen in your garden (the Feline Advisory Bureau has a good factsheet on this – visit www.fabcats.org), or by encouraging your cat to leave the house by an exit away from the traffic.

• **Are you allergic to cats?** Some people are fine with some cats but have a severe reaction to others. If you are allergic to fur or dander, spend a good amount of time with the cat you want to home before committing yourself, just to be sure.

• **Can you afford to have a cat?** Responsible cat owners will need to be able to pay for food, cat litter, etc, as well as annual vet-checks, neutering, and other health care.

You will see the occasional pedigree, such as this Siamese, among the amazing variety of cats in a rescue centre.
Photo: Tony Willitt

- **Do you own your home?** If you are in rented accommodation, do you have the landlord's permission to have pets? If you live in shared rental accommodation, where there is a frequent change in tenants, not everyone may like cats. If you are constantly moving to different shared accommodation, this might not be the right life for a cat, bearing in mind they can be territorial.

CHOOSING A CAT

So if you're sure that the cat is the pet for you, and that you can fulfil all his needs, what next? First, think about what type of cat you want.

What age?

Kittens are gorgeous. It's lovely to watch their clumsy ways and see them develop into agile, elegant adults. Young kittens will also be much more flexible behaviourally than adult cats, and will generally be more likely to accept new things that they come across as 'normal'. They will, for example, be easier to teach to get along with dogs, or to accept the noise and activity of young children. However, they do also involve more hard work. Most kittens will already be litter trained by the time that they are homed, but you will need to provide a litter tray, and make sure it is clean and accessible for the kitten. Kittens are also very energetic – they will need to spend a lot of time exploring and playing. If the sight of a kitten scaling your designer curtains would upset you, or you don't have the patience to deal with a kitten that wants to play with your socks when you're getting dressed in the morning, then consider a more sedate puss!

Adult cats can be easier if they are used to living in a household environment. They will usually be less demanding and energetic than kittens, and will mostly have established toileting habits. Problems may occur if an adult cat moves into an environment and comes across things he has never seen before.

Some cats can only be rehomed as indoor cats, due to health reasons, such as feline immunodeficiency virus (FIV). For one first-time cat owner, taking on one FIV boy – shortly followed by another – was one of the best decisions of her life...

When Veronica Risk from Larbert, Central Scotland, set up home with her partner, they decided to get a pet. Considering themselves primarily as 'dog people', they realised that they couldn't fulfil that ambition just yet, as their lifestyles were not compatible with the full-time commitment needed for dog ownership. So they looked into whether a cat would be the right pet for them, and decided that, yes, they could give a cat everything it needed.

After some research on the internet, Veronica found a gorgeous ginger tom – Henry – at Cats Protection's East Renfrewshire Branch. A home-visit was arranged, which was successful, and she then met Henry himself – an affectionate boy thought to be around eight

Hendrix: A new life as a house cat.

or nine years of age. It was love at first sight, and he was rehomed with Veronica, settling in quickly, and enjoying a new name of Hendrix.

Understanding FIV

It was only a matter of weeks before a routine blood-test, conducted at the vet's when he was being microchipped, revealed that Hendrix had FIV. Hearing that your cat has FIV can strike fear in the heart of any cat owner, but Veronica remained calm. She found out everything she could about the condition, and realised that things weren't as bad as she first thought.

"People can panic when they hear about 'feline AIDS', but it can't be passed on to people", Veronica explains.

"There is a risk of cross infection to other cats through a deep bite so it is necessary to keep affected cats indoors – for the affected cat's sake as much as anything else. It's important to protect FIV cats from infections from other cats or prey that might threaten their immune systems. So Veronica

and her dad set about making a large run for the garden.

Then, Veronica decided to get Hendrix a friend. Of course, to get around the problem of the small chance of him passing on the disease, it was necessary to get a companion that already had FIV. Another call to Cats Protection resulted in 18-month-old Sparky, now called Wizard, joining her family. Hendrix and Wizard get on incredibly well, and love to chase each other and play – both indoors and also out in their pen. They even enjoy walks on a harness.

Wild night

Veronica adores her two boys. "Hendrix loves full-body rubs and sleeps under the duvet on the bed," she says. "He's quieter than Wizard, but he does have his mad moments." One of these being when Veronica found that he had turned completely green one morning. He'd cracked into the catnip in the night and had enjoyed a wild night, rubbing himself all over in the 'drug'.

Young Wizard is completely

Wizard: He has learnt to enjoy outings on a harness.

because they are cared for so wonderfully. "They have a good diet, and I am careful not to give them any raw food; their inoculations are kept up to date, and they are given evening primrose and garlic supplements," Veronica explains. "It's also important to keep their teeth clean as bacteria can enter the body through gingivitis." Hendrix had a dental examination when Veronica got him, and she ensures that both her boys' teeth and gums are kept free of plaque and tartar.

crazy. "He's like a rocket; just mental; on a different planet," laughs Veronica. "He's like a dog, and loves to be chased! He enjoys playing with balls too."

Health-wise, both boys are in tip-top condition. "People imagine that they'll meet two half-dead cats, but that is far from the case," Veronica says. "Often it's only once a cat becomes ill that the owners will screen for FIV, but the cat could have lived with the condition for ten years or so before then."

The immune systems of FIV cats can be compromised, but all tests on Hendrix and Wizard show their levels to be in the normal ranges – probably

No regrets

It's been nearly 18 months since Hendrix and then Wizard joined Veronica, and she has no regrets about giving her home and heart to her FIV felines.

"They mean everything to me, and I wouldn't change them for the world. I would recommend FIV cats to anyone – especially those wanting indoor cats, as they are ideal. Oh, and yes… I am now a 100 per cent signed-up cat lover!"

An adult becomes less flexible, and more likely to be fearful of new objects or experiences. Oldies make particularly affectionate companions, and are sadly often overlooked in rehoming centres, although they have so much to offer (see page 93). Remember, many cats live well into their teens, staying agile and playful for much of their lives, so don't overlook the older cat – he may be just the right one for you.

Male or female?

This is another personal preference. Some people always have female cats; for others, males are supreme. Really, once a cat is neutered, there are no real differences between the sexes, and it is impossible to make generalisations, as every cat is different. It depends on the individual cat and your own family dynamics (such as any existing cats' personalities).

Moggie or purebred?

Unlike in the world of dogs, most cats are not purebred.

Pedigree breeds have a committed following, but most people only know a handful of names, and apart from the Siamese and Persian, population numbers are fairly low.

If you are interested in a pedigree cat, then research the breed's needs (via the internet, breeders, clubs, or books). One may turn up in a rescue centre, but you will probably have to wait a long while. Alternatively, contact the relevant breed club, who may be able to put you in contact with a specialist rescue co-ordinator.

Since the majority of cats are similar in looks, size, temperament and conformation (unlike dogs, where vast differences can be seen), most true cat enthusiasts love all cats, regardless of breed or looks.

In or out?

In some circumstances, cats need to be kept indoors for their health or welfare. However, such cats require more stimulation, as they need the mental and physical exercise they would otherwise get from hunting, stalking leaves and climbing trees. An indoor cat needs plenty of 'enrichment', just as a lion or tiger would do in a zoo. Encouraging your cat to use the whole space of your home is important – you can do this with a 'cat tree', or by providing high shelves, or ways up onto existing pieces of furniture. This is particularly important if you have more than one cat, as they sometimes like to be able to get past each other on different 'levels'.

You will also need to provide lots of opportunity for play – this can be through directly playing with him with toys, and by providing toys that he can play with himself. About half of cats respond to catnip, so this can be used to entertain these individuals.

Rather than providing an indoor cat with all of his food in a bowl, it is a good idea to use 'puzzle feeders' for some dry food, which he needs to move around in order to get the pieces of food to drop out.

This will mean that your cat is using up more of his time and energy in getting his food than just tucking into a bowl. You can also grow cat grass for him to nibble on, as this will help his digestion as well as providing him with more interest in his environment.

In most cases cats that 'grow up' in an indoor environment as kittens cope better with this situation than those that have previously been outside and are then restricted.

Coat type

Do you mind what length of coat the cat has, or what colour he is? Long-haired and semi-long pusses look very glamorous, but they do need frequent grooming. If you don't realistically have the time to commit to this, then opt for a short-haired cat.

Coat colour is a personal matter. If you have a 'thing' for tabbies, have always fancied a tortoiseshell, or would prefer to avoid a white cat because it reminds you of a cat you have

recently lost, then let the rescue centre know your preferences. However, being choosy about the look of your cat may mean you'll have to wait for the right one to come up, depending on what's available when you arrive. It is better to think about the type or personality of cat that would best suit your lifestyle rather than focusing too much on appearance.

WHERE TO GO

So you now know what type of cat you would like, but where do you go to find one? There are many reputable rehoming organisations – either small, local charities, or large, national ones, such as Cats Protection, with Branches across the country. Whichever one you choose, consider the following:

- Are the premises and cat pens clean?

- The litter trays and bowls should be clean, and there should be scratching facilities, a warm, cosy bed for each cat, and perhaps a toy.
- Do the cats look happy and well cared for?
- You should be asked lots of questions about yourself, your family and your lifestyle.
- Are the staff or volunteers affectionate towards the cats, and knowledgeable about each individual's case, character and needs?

You might also want to consider the organisation's policies. For example, some charities, such as Cats Protection, operate a non-destruction policy, where no healthy cat is ever put to sleep. Other organisations euthanase longer-stay residents – cats that haven't found a home through them within a fixed period of time – to make way for new cats coming in. You could even investigate how the charity spends its money, and its aims as outlined in a mission statement.

To find rescue centres in your area, consult your local telephone directory, use a reliable internet search engine, or contact a local vet practice.

THE CHARITIES

Cats Protection

Cats Protection is the UK's leading cat welfare charity, rehoming around 60,000 cats each year through its nationwide network of 29 Adoption Centres and 260 voluntary-run Branches. Cats Protection also promotes the benefits of neutering for a happy and healthy pet, and produces a wealth of cat care information to encourage responsible pet ownership. It never puts a healthy cat to sleep.

The Blue Cross

This charity provides practical support, information and advice for pet and horse owners. Through its network of animal adoption centres it rehomes around 3,000 cats per year. Its hospitals provide veterinary care

The cats at a rescue centre should be kept in clean, hygienic conditions.

for the pets of people who cannot afford private vets' fees. Each cat will leave The Blue Cross having been micro-chipped, neutered and vaccinated.

Wood Green Animal Shelters

Wood Green Animal Shelters is a registered charity that has been rescuing and rehoming animals since 1924. The charity rehomes 3,500 animals a year and has set national standards in animal care. It has three shelters: in London, Heydon (Herts) and Godmanchester (Cambs).

Battersea Dogs and Cats Home

Few people knew that Battersea has been rehoming cats since 1883, so the charity changed its name! There are usually 100 cats in the home, rising to 150 at very busy times, with around 2,100 being rehomed each year. The charity's aims are to: "rescue, reunite and rehabilitate and rehome the lost and abandoned dogs and cats that come into [its] care."

RSPCA

Established in 1824, the RSPCA aims to promote kindness to all animals (including pets and wildlife) and works to prevent and suppress cruelty to animals. The charity rehomes in the region of 33,000 cats each year, and has a network of 15 animal centres, 38 branches, nine animal welfare centres, four hospitals and five clinics across the country.

SSPCA

The Scottish SPCA (an independent charity to the RSPCA) has been caring for, and striving to prevent cruelty to, Scotland's animals since 1839. Every year, its 13 animal welfare centres offer refuge to more than 15,000 injured, abused and neglected pets, farm animals and wildlife; of this figure, it takes in around 2,400 cats each year. Cats are microchipped before rehoming, and, at selected centres, are neutered free of charge.

THE PROCESS OF ADOPTION

A reputable centre may want to see you in your home

environment. The purpose of a home-visit is to gain as much information as possible about your lifestyle, to increase the chances of finding a suitable match of cat and home. For example, is your dog quiet or bouncy? Do you live in a cul-de-sac or on a busy road? Will the cat be on his own for extended periods?

The home-visit may be done before or after you have chosen a specific cat. They are very informal – there's no need to spend hours cleaning your home beforehand! The home-visitor isn't interested in how much dust you have on your TV but will be wanting to assess which type of cat will best suit you and your family. For example, they may want to talk to you about:

• The environment around your home, such as the number of other cats already in the neighbourhood.
• The home itself – if you live in a ground floor flat, what garden facilities are there for the puss? If you live in an

Sometimes companion cats need rehoming – and this is an ideal choice if you have room for more than one cat.

Photo: Lady Musker

upper flat, with no outdoor access for the cat, are you aware of how best to care for a house-cat? Are the windows secure? Can balconies be kept out of bounds?

- The size of your home. Cats are territorial and need their personal space. As a general rule, an average three-bedroomed house will accommodate two moggies. Larger numbers can result in stress, which will affect the welfare of your cat and may also lead to a number of different behaviour problems.
- Your other pets – do they seem confident, friendly, and willing to accept a newcomer?
- The make-up of your family – some types of cats or kittens will cope better with young children than cats of a more nervous disposition.

In some cases, it may be that the charity considers that your environment or circumstances are not suitable for any of the cats that they currently have. If this happens, do not take it personally. You will be told why this is the case and may need to wait for a suitable cat to become available, or for other circumstances to change. Do not rush out to buy a kitten from a newspaper advert or elsewhere – the welfare organisation that conducted the assessment has only the cat's best interests at heart. It is best to wait until the right match becomes available.

MEETING THE CATS

Some charities, such as Cats Protection, have large, staffed Adoption Centres across the country as well as many regional Branches run by volunteers. If you live near a main centre, then you can visit and see all the cats that need rehoming. Do bear in mind that it's not a case of just picking the one you like the look of – some may have special characteristics that make them unsuitable for your home or family. The centre staff will guide you.

If you are not close to an Adoption Centre, then your nearest Branch can give you details of what cats are available at the time, and an opportunity to meet those who may fit in with your home and family.

Some charities allow you to take the cat straightaway, provided the cat is healthy and you are prepared at home (having cat-proofed and shopped for the newcomer – page 31). If this is the case, then take along a suitable carrier (not cardboard) to transport him home (page 51).

If you have young children, take them with you, so that you can see whether the cat interacts well with them.

When you meet the cats, be quiet and gentle. Remember that they are in an alien environment, which can be stressful for them. Plus, they now have a stranger to deal with. If the cat approaches you, slowly offer a hand for him to sniff, or gently stroke him around the side of his face or under the chin. Remember: a

Take time to assess the cat's personality, and consider whether he will fit in with your family set-up.

Photo: Paul Keevil

slow blink from you is a smile to a cat! Within a few minutes, you will get a sense of his character, but remember that the circumstances are somewhat artificial. Yes, if a cat is bold in a pen, then he is likely to be bold at home. But a shy, nervous cat in a pen may be confident in a secure, loving home once he's settled in.

If a cat backs away from you in his pen, try not to keep reaching out for him, as this will tend to make him feel nervous or defensive. Cats that do not appear to be friendly in this environment can often become great pets, so allow lots of time and be patient when first making friends.

Think about whether you want one cat or can consider two. Two who get on together can provide company for each other – and amusement for you as they play.

Sometimes it's a case of love at first sight for both parties. Some cats may be off-ish with some people but then go into raptures of purrs and cuddles for one individual. Often this is because the person reminds them of someone they once loved.

You should be told about each cat – his history (if known), approximate age, any health problems, and personality. The carers should have a good idea of each cat's character and will know if they are suitable for your home and family. Don't be afraid to ask questions in order to find out as much as possible about the cats you are looking at.

FINAL STEP

When you have found the cat for you, and provided his rehoming profile matches what you can offer, then it's a case of dealing with the paperwork.

Each charity will have a slightly different procedure, but generally it involves:

- Making a donation to help towards the cost of the cat's care and veterinary treatment.
- Filling out a form, giving your details and the cat's.
- Being given the veterinary paperwork (details of worming, vaccination, microchipping and neutering), and providing details of your own vet.
- Having a 'hand-over' chat to give general advice, or you may be given a series of leaflets outlining feeding and grooming requirements, plus general care and training advice.
- Many organisations reserve the right to make a home-visit at any point in the future (usually within six months to a year) in order to check on the cat's welfare and progress. You will be asked to sign your agreement to this, and/or any other regulations.

Photo: David Hudson

CHAPTER TWO

GETTING READY

Before you bring your new puss home, it's important to make sure that your home and garden are safe. Cats are notoriously curious, but this can lead to accidents or even tragedy. Be safe not sorry!

The home-visitor will have raised any concerns with you, which should be addressed, but here are some more pointers to consider.

INDOORS

- Go through the house, room by room. Crawl around on the floor to view things from a cat's perspective. For example, you might see an otherwise hidden electrical cable dangling down behind a table, which could tempt a playful cat or kitten.
- Cats like small, warm, dark nooks and crannies. An open door to a tumble-dryer or washing machine is a welcome invitation to a puss on the look-out for a new place to nap. All such appliances should be checked before closing the door, just in case the cat has nipped inside.
- If your cooker has a hob lid, always put it down after cooking, as the rings may remain warm for some time and burn a cat's paws

(especially if the cooker is electric).

- The toilet lid should always be put down after use. Cats have been known to drown by falling into the bowl, and can be poisoned if they lick water with bleach or other cleaning agents in it.
- If you run a bath, shut the cat out of the room whilst you are not in it. Some cats are fascinated by running water, but if he slips into a hot bath, he could be scalded and unable to get out.
- Think of your cat like a toddler – keep medicines, cleaning chemicals, sharp objects (knives, needles), glass/fragile items, plastic bags and so on out of reach in a cupboard. Some cats can open cupboards (or even fridges!), so think about installing childproof catches.
- Cats are renowned for being agile and sure-footed – but they can be surprisingly clumsy! Ornaments can get knocked over and broken, so keep them safely in a display cabinet. Vases with water should be removed in case they get knocked over and spill on to electrical equipment or stain wood or carpets.
- Make sure your stairs are well lit, and get into the habit of turning on the light before going up or down. Cats tend to sleep in the most awkward of places, and, being good vantage points, stairs and landings are often chosen.
- When you clean, remember to rinse any residue chemicals away thoroughly. Cleaning the kitchen floor in a bleach solution, for example, can be dangerous as the cat will get the chemical on his paws and then lick it off when he grooms. The same applies to sink and bath mousses, or surface cleaners such as anti-bacterial wipes.
- Ensure any house plants are non-toxic to cats. Most moggies will avoid anything harmful, but some don't have much safety sense! For a list of dangerous plants (indoors

Cats are intrepid explorers, and you need to double check that your home is free from potential hazards.
Photo: Roy Bolton

and out), visit the Feline Advisory Bureau website www.fabcats.org/hiddendangersofplants.html

- Open chimneys are especially risky with kittens or nervous cats in the house. All fires (gas, electric, wood, coal) should be fitted with guards.

OUTDOORS

It's important that your garden is safe, too. Although you can't prevent your cat from wandering off into other people's gardens (unless you build a large enclosure), if you make your own garden safe, with everything he'll need, the more time he will spend in it.

- In the same way that you must train yourself (and family members) always to remember to check the washing machine before closing the door, so you must be mindful of accidentally shutting the cat in a shed or garage.
- Make sure all garden chemicals are safely out of harm's way. Don't use slug

pellets or other pesticides, unless they are clearly marked as being non-toxic to pets.

- Cover garden ponds or swimming pools when you are not enjoying them, in case a cat slips in and cannot get out. (However, do ensure that any net used is not a hazard to hedgehogs and other wildlife.)

- Ensure there are no spills of antifreeze, which is toxic to cats.

- Tip: prickly bushes grown next to fences will help to confine your cat to your garden.

WELCOMING TOUCHES
Now, you can start to make your home and garden not just cat-safe but cat-friendly.

Garden Retreat
- Cats love to nibble grass and it is essential for their health, preventing fur balls and

The best plan is to cover swimming pools and paddling pools when you are not using them.
Photo: Vanessa Clarke

Scratching is a natural activity for all cats. It gives the opportunity to stretch, to mark territory, and remove claw husks.

Photo: Angela Smart

FLOWER POWER

- To prevent your cat from ruining your garden with his toilet excavations, provide him with his own area (see Outdoor Loo, opposite).
- Chicken manure is a great cat-deterrent for flowerbeds. Cats hate the smell of the manure, and it can also encourage established plants to grow (although care should be taken with tender plants, as excess nitrogen burns them). Use pellets approved by the Soil Association.
- Stone chippings or large pebbles will also keep puss away, as he won't like walking on them – and they act as weed suppressants!
- If your cat tries to toilet inside a plant container, top the soil up with large stones.

relieving bile. Cocksfoot grass (*Dactylis glomerata*) is particularly favoured and can be grown easily – indoors or out. (Cats Protection supplies the seeds if you have difficulty getting hold of them.)

• Another great planting choice is fresh catnip (*Nepeta cataria*). Although some cats aren't fussed by it, many go crazy for the stuff, rolling in it, playing with it, nibbling it and generally having a mad five minutes. Not only will it be enjoyed by your cat, but it will provide hours of amusement as you watch him! It can also be cut and dried, and then used to stuff small toys.

• Provide an outdoor scratching area; this will give him plenty of opportunities to stretch, mark his territory, and remove his claw husks, as well as encouraging him away from delicate shrubs and trees. An

OUTDOOR LOO

Even with access to an indoor litter tray, many cats prefer to toilet outside during the day. To prevent your bulbs being unearthed, or your puss making a nuisance of himself in your neighbours' gardens, provide an allocated toileting spot for him to use.

• Find a secluded, sheltered area in your garden, such as under some thick vegetation.

• Pour a bag of compost on the area you want your cat to use and he won't go anywhere else!

• Alternatively, dig and hoe the soil, so that it is fine and well drained.

• Add some of your own cat's lightly-soiled litter initially, to encourage him to use it; he should recognise the scent and realise that this is his outdoor loo.

• If your cat doesn't like getting his paws muddy, then cover the area in bark or add some fresh peat.

• Turn the soil over regularly, to keep it hygienic and to encourage the soiled material to decompose naturally.

old wooden post will do the job nicely.

- Cats are natural sun-worshippers, but they are just as prone to the harmful rays as humans are (see page 99), so make sure there is a shady spot where he can snooze. A place under established bushes, away from prickles or thorns, will offer welcome relief from the sun.
- A decorative pebble pool or fountain can provide amusement for those who like dipping their paws in water, trying to catch it! This may also encourage your cat to drink enough too, as cats often prefer to sip from running water.
- If you have a cat-flap in your door, try and make sure that there is some cover for your cat on the outside. Cats often feel very vulnerable popping through a hole into a wide open space, and will be grateful for a few plant pots around the door to help them feel secure.
- Bird tables are asking for trouble – it's best not to encourage birds to your garden, as the temptation may be too great for your puss. If you wish to feed the birds, locate hanging feeders well out of your cat's reach.

Home sweet home

Now, turn your attentions to your home. When cats feel threatened, they like to hide in small, cosy spaces (the airing cupboard, under the bed, etc.) You need to recreate this kind of environment to help him feel safe when he first arrives in your home. Hiding is a normal behaviour for cats when they are scared, so make sure that there is opportunity for him to cope in this way. A small, quiet room is best for your cat's first introduction to the house, but if you need to use a large, open room, make it less scary by putting in some cardboard boxes that he can climb inside. The room that you first bring your cat into should also contain your cat's bed, the litter tray, a scratching post, a food

A box can be useful for the settling-in period.

Photo: Anna Burgon

and water bowl (not close to the tray), and some toys.

Being able to recognise his own scent in his surroundings will help a cat to feel at home, so if possible bring home something, e.g. a toy from the rescue centre that already carries your cat's own smell. You will recognise when your new cat starts to feel more comfortable in his new environment, as he will start to put his own scent on to new objects by rubbing against doors, chairs, etc to cover the area with his facial pheromones. You can stroke him with a dry cloth or flannel, paying particular attention to the sides of his mouth (most cats love being rubbed here), and then you can rub the cloth around his cat room at cat-head height to help speed up this process.

If it is not possible to bring home something that already smells of your cat, a commercial pheromone diffuser or spray may help puss to settle more quickly in his new home, particularly if he is fearful. This commercial product is a synthetic version of the generic basis of the cats' facial pheromone – it is unlikely to be as successful as the cat's own scent, but can be more convenient to use. Synthetic pheromones are available from your veterinary surgeon.

The pen den

These are metal mesh, collapsible pens (also known as 'crates'), often used for puppy training and for transporting dogs – although they can be a valuable asset for settling in a kitten or cat too. Place a blanket over the top, and let it drape over the back and sides, leaving the front open. Line the bottom with an old blanket or towel, and put your cat's things inside. The door should be left open for the cat to come and go at will, but it will provide an area where he will feel comfortable and secure, and this will encourage him to start venturing further afield, investigating his new home (see page 56).

Cat-flap

Before bringing your cat home, you may want to install a cat-flap ready for his first excursions outside in a few weeks' time. It can be put through a door, or even through a wall, window or patio door glass. Wherever it is placed, make sure it is not too high – he should be able to walk through without a struggle.

There is a very wide selection available – some with matching magnetic collars, which open the flap for the wearer, but bar access to other neighbourhood cats. This can be advantageous where other cats are making your cat feel insecure, although problems can arise if, for example, other cats follow your puss inside and then get trapped there with them. In addition, be careful about the type of collar you fit on a cat – it should be one that will release should he get caught up.

Whichever type of cat-flap you choose, ensure that it is lockable. At night, or during firework season, or if puss is ill,

Your cat will appreciate a bed – but will soon find his favourite rest spots.
Photo: Betty Chadwick

you will want to be able to keep him inside. Be warned: some smart cats can unlock flaps, learning that if it is locked to prevent him going out, but not coming back in, then he can hook his claws under the flap and pull it inwards towards him, before squeezing through. And if a new cat panics, he may break through a double-locked flap, as he will smell the fresh air and will attempt to escape. So you must ensure your cat cannot gain access to the room with the flap when he is to be kept indoors, or that the cat-flap is safely blocked by some other means (such as having a piece of hardboard tacked over it).

SHOPPING LIST

Cats aren't expensive pets, needing only some basic accessories to keep them happy.

Bed

A snug bed in his 'safe room' will be a welcome retreat – somewhere to snooze undisturbed. A hidey-hole type of bed will be especially appreciated in the early days of bringing him home. A cardboard box with a blanket in the bottom and a small entrance door cut out at the front is as good as any hooded cat bed you can buy, and can be replaced cheaply, should he decide to use it as a scratching post (or litter tray!) instead.

Be warned: however much effort – or expense – you go to, puss may well abandon his bed once he settles in, and will probably choose his own snooze spots around the house. Many cats have a favourite cushion on the sofa, as well as colonising a windowsill, a square foot of a human bed, the laundry basket, and so on! Don't be surprised if he ends up with a 'bed' in every room!

Bowls

You will need two for food (one for wet food, one for biscuit) and one for water (and, ideally, a spare set – so six bowls in all). However much you are enticed

A feeding bowl should be wide and shallow – and easy to clean.
Photo: Patricia Lam

by pretty design and decoration, make sure the bowl is functional. Most cats prefer wide, shallow bowls, rather than deep, narrow ones, as they do not like their whiskers to touch the sides of a bowl when eating or drinking. Some cats do not like plastic or metal dishes as these can affect the taste of the food. Make sure that you have a food and water bowl for each cat within the household in a multi-cat house. These should be put in different parts of the house to ensure that each cat can easily access them without being restricted by other cats.

Litter tray

These come in two types – the standard, open tray, and the covered variety, which may also have a flap for access. Both have their pros and cons. The open trays are cheap, easily cleaned, and simple for the cat to use when he's first learning about litter-training. Make sure it is deep enough to have a good covering of litter, but not so deep that he will sink into it and feel overwhelmed. A shallow one is fine for a kitten, but move up to a deeper one when he is adult. Oldies may need to revert to a shallow tray if they are suffering from arthritis.

The covered trays can make cats feel more secure when toileting, although this is not always the case, as they can be wary of using them if they are ambushed by another cat on coming out of the flap! These types of trays can also build up a smell more quickly for the cat, and fastidious cats can avoid using them for this reason. With young cats that may not be familiar with cat-flaps, they may prefer to choose their own toileting area rather than messing around with pushing open the door to the tray.

Any litter tray should be placed somewhere quiet and out of the way. It should be in a place where a cat is not overlooked by other cats, nor in a busy place where he will be disturbed whilst toileting.

In a multi-cat household, it is important to ensure that you have as many litter trays as cats

You will be spoiled for choice when you go toy shopping, or you can try your hand at making some fun cat toys.

Photo: Chris Tims

– in addition these should be distributed around the house. Putting a load of litter trays in a row in the utility room won't help a fearful cat that is worried about coming downstairs!

Cat litter

Stock up on a couple of bags of cat litter before bringing your new puss home. Ask the rescue centre what type the cat is used to, as it will help him to recognise his toileting area more easily once he is with you. Avoid scented litter, as it can irritate cats. If the litter tray smells, don't mask the scent with deodorants – clean the tray more regularly. For more information, see page 53.

Toys

This is the fun bit of shopping for a cat! There are thousands of cat toys on the market, ranging from cheap bits of plastic to remote-controlled mice and huge multi-play activity centres. Cats vary a great deal in their tastes. Where one cat may leap with joy at a jingly bell ball, another will dive for cover, hating the noise! Some love large fluffy rats to 'kill'; others are wimpy and prefer to 'hunt' tiny mice. Your cat will soon let you know what he enjoys – until you know, don't spend a fortune on expensive gadgets and games.

If you do buy toys that are suspended at the end of elastic or string, do not leave the cat alone with them, as he may get entangled and panic.

Cats often love to chase ping-pong balls. Long feathers (e.g. ostrich or peacock feathers) are great toys, too, as they are soft, so can't hurt the cat's mouth, and they keep your fingers well away from his claws and teeth!

Remember: your hands are not toys! If you encourage your cat to wrestle with your hands (e.g. if you tickle his tummy), you are teaching him that it is okay to bite and scratch your hands – so don't blame him if it hurts!

Of course, home-made toys are just as enjoyable. A screwed-up lottery ticket can be chased around the kitchen floor for hours (make sure it's not a winning ticket, though!). It will be flicked up in the air and then pounced on, then batted under the fridge before being hooked out to be chased

---

CHIP TIP

Some owners prefer to rely on microchipping as a permanent, safe means of identification.

Microchipping is where a chip – about the size of a grain of rice and coded with the owner's details – is inserted by a vet, or other qualified professional, under the skin, between the shoulder blades. Many cats from charities have already been microchipped.

again... Use your imagination, and just have fun together!

Of course, to many cats, the best toy in the world is one with a human on the other end of it!

Collar

Although a collar is meant to safeguard a cat and ensure he is returned to you if he gets lost, a number of cats are seriously injured – some killed – by collars every year. So, what is a 'safe' collar? You must be able to slip two fingers under the collar at right angles to his neck to ensure that the collar is slack enough to come off his neck in an emergency. However, don't fit the collar too loose or the cat may get his foot or even lower jaw caught in it (when grooming). Ideally, choose a collar with a catch that snaps apart when it gets caught on something. The advantage of a safe collar with identifying details is that people can reunite you with the cat should he become lost,

without having to take him to a vet surgery or rehoming centre equipped with a microchip scanner.

Cat carrying basket

A sturdy carrying box or basket (preferably not cardboard) is important for transporting your cat home, to a cattery or to the vet.

VET SEARCH

When you get your new cat home, you should register with a nearby vet surgery. If the cat has come from a reputable rescue centre, he would have been seen by a vet recently, so a hands-on visit is not always necessary – just registering by phone should suffice.

If you aren't already registered somewhere, here are some things to consider in your search for a vet:

- Surgeries can be small-animal practices (cats, dogs, and other small pets), equine (horses only), large-animal practices (farm animals), or mixed (both pets and farm

The vet may be an important person in your cat's life, so take time to find a cat-friendly and people-friendly practice.

Photo: Paul Keevil

stock). Within practices, vets may specialise in certain areas. Often, a vet who specialises in small animals is a good choice, as he or she will be better practised in this field.

- How are appointments arranged? Is it a 'turn up and wait' system, can you phone up for a fixed appointment, or is it a mixture of the two? What best suits your daily schedule?

- Is the clinic clean, with welcoming staff, and adequate waiting-room space (a cat in a basket won't want to be leapt on by a dog, or be jammed next to another hissing cat in a basket). An allocated 'cat corner' is an advantage.

- What services can the practice provide? Some have regular clinics where specialists visit – cardiologists, dermatologists, opthalmologists, etc. Most run weight-loss and veteran clinics in-house.

- Is the clinic easy for you to get to, with good parking facilities? Or is it on a regular public transport route?

- What are the arrangements for out-of-hours emergencies? All vets must make provision for 24-hour care, but they differ in how it is provided. Some vets have a rota system where one of their own vets is on call at night; some other practices link up with other vet surgeries. In the case of the latter, make sure you know where this clinic is (it may be a considerable distance from your home, in an unfamiliar area).

- What facilities does the practice have? Some are better equipped than others, offering a good range of on-site testing for quicker diagnoses (in other cases, samples have to be sent away to a lab, with an obvious time delay).

- What's your gut instinct? In some cases, you might gel instantly with a vet, or you may just not feel happy with the clinic. Trust your judgement: you must have a good rapport with the vet and have confidence in his or her abilities.

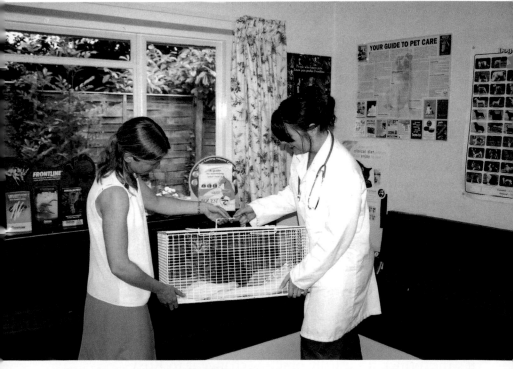

Check out the facilities offered at your local veterinary practice.
Photo: Cats Protection

You may need to think up a name for your new arrival.

Photo: Sandra Price

CHOOSING A NAME

Your rescued cat may already have a name – either one he's lived with for years with a previous owner or one given to him by the rehoming staff. If it's the former, it's usually best to keep it, as he will be used to it. If you really don't like the name, then choose one that sounds very similar. For example, if a female cat has been called a butch-sounding Rocky, you might want to change it to Roxy.

If the cat was unhappy in his

previous home (such as through abuse or neglect), he may have only negative connotations with his name, so you should consider changing it completely. This only applies to a small percentage of rescued cats.

If a cat's name is not known, and he has been named by rehoming staff, he is unlikely to have become accustomed to his name (depending on the length of time he has been waiting for a home). You can stick with the name, or choose another one entirely.

Often, a cat's name emerges once you get to know him, and the name you first chose may seem entirely inappropriate. Within a couple of weeks, you should be able to find one that is suitable.

Whatever name you choose, remember that you will end up calling it a lot from your back door!

If the children want to call him La-la or Tinky Winky, after their favourite Teletubby, are you happy for your neighbours to hear you yelling this ad infinitum to get puss in at night?

Remember too that the kids will outgrow Teletubbies, but your cat will be stuck with the name for his lifetime!

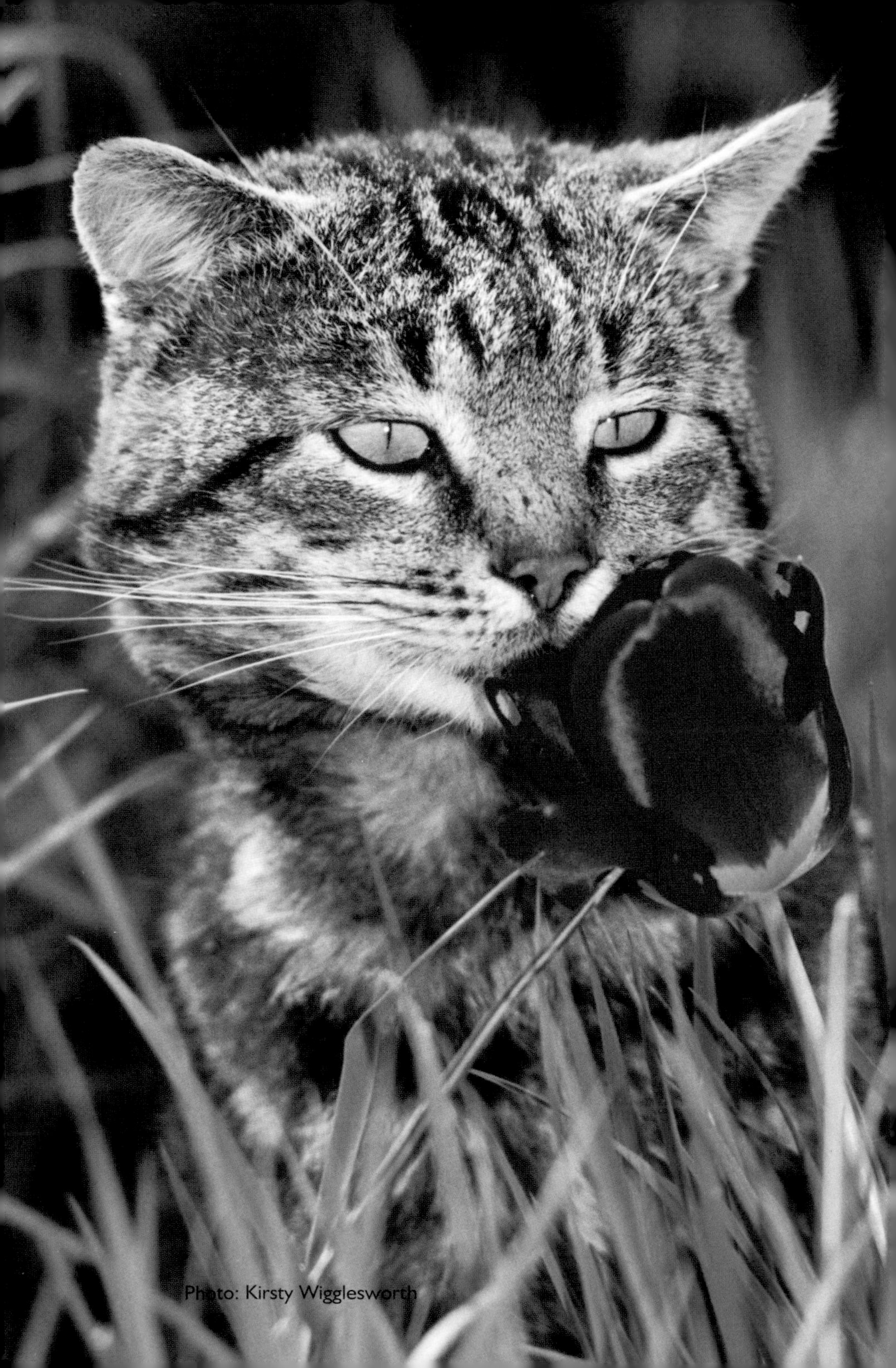
Photo: Kirsty Wigglesworth

CHAPTER THREE

SETTLING IN

After all your planning and preparations, the day has finally arrived for collecting your new puss and bringing him home. Take along a secure cat carrier (preferably plastic or wire), with some newspaper and a towel or blanket in the bottom, to make it cosy for his journey home, and to absorb any accidents should they occur. Also take along any paperwork you have been asked for (some organisations may ask for a reference from a vet, for example), as well as a method of payment. Most charities ask for a donation – some have a fixed amount, others ask for whatever you can afford.

A secure cat carrier will be needed to transport your cat.

At last the waiting is over, and it is time to bring your cat home.
Photo: Paul Keevil

Once you have sorted out all the paperwork, signing documents promising to care for the cat and agreeing to future home-visits etc, make sure that you ask any questions you may have about looking after the cat. You should also be given a telephone number to call should you encounter any problems.

JOURNEY HOME
Then it's home time! With the cat in the carrier, put it in a safe area of the car (such as in the footwell), or perhaps on the back seat, with the seatbelts holding the carrier securely in place.

If you are driving, try to avoid putting the basket on the passenger seat next to you; some cats are determined to get your attention and poke their paws through the carrier. It can be very disconcerting to change gear and be grabbed by a cat; unhooking a cat's claws from your clothes whilst driving is not something recommended in the Highway Code.

If you have taken a friend or family member with you, then they can sit in the back with the cat basket next to them, to check puss is okay and to quietly talk to him, giving reassurance for the journey home.

Be prepared for some yowling. Some cats really don't like travelling in the car, and are not reticent about expressing their displeasure.

Cats are pretty smart when it comes to litter training – usually it's just a case of showing them the litter tray and letting them get on with it! New cat owners, especially if they have had puppies in the past, are usually amazed at how quickly a kitten or older cat is house-trained. Kittens learn to associate going to the toilet with the material that is under their feet when they are very tiny kittens. They learn this because their mother will move them to a suitable toileting site and stimulate them to toilet through licking their rear end. The kitten rapidly forms a preference for toileting on that type of surface, and will generally prefer this material throughout life.

The location of the litter tray is crucial to ensuring that cats are able to find it on arriving at your house. Puss must feel safe when using the tray, so place it in a corner of his cat room initially (but away from his bed and food bowls), and then in a quiet corner of the house, away from the usual household 'traffic' and other pets.

The type of litter is also important. At first, it is essential to use the same type that the cat is used to (remember that they have a strong preference): the rescue centre will be able to tell you what type of litter he has been happy to use.

Grains

If you really want to change the type of litter later, you can do this, but it must be done very gradually, by slowly adding progressively more and more of the new litter material and less and less of the old. Generally, cats prefer fine grains to the larger pellets (the latter can be uncomfortable for them to stand on, or to dig).

Keep the tray clean. Cats hate to use dirty trays, so scoop out any deposits as soon as they are left, and change the litter entirely twice a week. Clean the tray with a specific cat disinfectant from pet stores, as others may be poisonous to cats, and rinse in boiling water at least once a week. Dry it and then refill with clean litter. If you have more than one cat, the trays will need changing and cleaning more frequently, and remember that you should definitely be providing as many trays as there are cats, and spreading them in different places around the house. When he is going outside, don't dispense with the tray. He will still need it at night, when he is kept inside, and some cats prefer to continue using the tray even in the daytime (coming inside to toilet before returning outside once more).

Scented

Once you've scooped out the clumps of urine or other deposits, what do you do with them? In some homes, it can be flushed down the toilet, but many plumbing systems won't cope with the inevitable build-up of litter.

A good tip is to keep a box of scented nappy sacks or dog scoop bags by the tray. You can either put your hand in the bag and pick up the deposit, and

then turn the bag inside out and tie it, before placing it in the bin, or you can use the scoop and place the contents in the bag before tying it.

If accidents do happen, there's always a good reason. Cats don't suddenly change their toileting habits for no reason, so if your cat starts to toilet away from the litter box, you need to consider why it is that the litter tray is no longer acceptable for him. This may be because:

- The litter material you are using does not match his preference for a toileting surface.
- The litter tray may be too small, or have sides that are too high for him.
- The litter tray may not be cleaned frequently enough, or conversely, you may be cleaning it so much that there is no scent of urine to attract him there.
- The litter tray may not be in a place where he feels safe and secure enough to toilet. The presence of a dog, people, or other cats will often prevent cats from using their litter tray.

- He cannot get to the area where the litter tray is, for example because he is inhibited by another cat, or may be inhibited by the presence of people if he is a nervous cat.

Once a cat has soiled away from the litter tray, the scent of this will often attract him back to use the same location again. To avoid this, you need to clean the area very thoroughly with a biologically active cleaner (available from your vet), or a ten per cent solution of biological washing powder.

A good reason

Changes in toileting behaviour are relatively common in cats. If it does occur with your cat remember that there is a good reason for him to do so from his point of view. It is important not to get angry with him or shout at or punish him, as this will most likely make the situation worse, and make the cat scared of you too.

Cats that change their pattern of toileting should be checked over by a vet – there are a number of medical conditions that can cause this, and it is essential to eliminate these before assuming the change is behavioural. Where no medical problem is found, your vet should be able to refer you to a suitably qualified behaviour specialist to advise you about changing your cats inappropriate behaviour. See also page 108.

Cats are naturally clean and fastidious, and it will not take long before your cat gets the idea of litter training.
Photo: John Barnes

ARRIVING HOME

Before bringing puss into your home, check that any other pets you have are not in the designated cat room (page 37). Then take your cat to the room, close the door, open the carrier door and let him wander out in his own good time. He will make tentative steps out of the basket, and will probably find a corner to hide in, but don't hassle him. If he's nervous and wants to hide, then leave him to it for a while.

Check on him in an hour's time – kneel on the floor and speak to him softly. If he comes up for a cuddle, great! If he's not ready yet, leave him for longer. Never force him out of any hiding places – he's there because he doesn't feel confident. Dragging him out will only increase his stress.

With patience, puss will soon be investigating his room – maybe having a mouthful of food and a drink, and using his litter tray. He may even start to play with any toys left out for him.

Some cats are bold and confident, and will march out of the carrier, look around and feel they own the place within minutes. Others may take a few days to be fully settled in their cat room.

It may take time before your cat feels confident with his new family.
Photo: Simon Parker

Finding themselves in a new home, most cats are timid to start off with, but with time and patience, the majority blossom into confident and loving companions.

Janet Neville has been a volunteer at Cat Protection's Evesham Adoption Centre for 21 years. During this time she has helped to socialise many kittens – even those born feral. One of the most recent, Hattie, was too nervous to be rehomed to the general public, and so Janet kept her.

"Initially there were two 15-week-old kittens," says Janet. "But Hattie's brother, James, came round so quickly that he was rehomed. It's good to get the kittens used to life inside the home – the sound of the washing machine or vacuum cleaner, and usual hectic family life. I have a utility area with the cats' beds and litter trays in, and the cats usually spend time in there until they are brave enough to venture into the rest of the house.

" James came out quite quickly – he wasn't fazed at all, but Hattie wasn't confident for months. We just let her settle in, in her own time. We made sure she was fed and cared for, but then just let her be. My eldest daughter, Sara, then 16 years, would sit in the room quietly with Hattie and would cuddle her if she wanted attention.

"When James went, Hattie became more nervous for a while. She had used James to hide behind."

Eventually, however, Hattie's confidence grew and she ventured out of the utility area after about four months, and although she remained skittish of loud or sudden noises, her trust in her family meant she would approach Janet, her husband and her three children for attention. Still, three years on, Hattie is nervous around people outside her family, but she's happy and anxiety-free in 'her' garden, with her loved ones, and with the dog and other two cats in the house.

"She's so confident now, in her own surroundings, that you would never know that she'd started life as a feral kitten," says Janet.

Surprise change

Some turnarounds can be even more surprising. One of Janet's other cats, Diana, was aged between six and 12 months when she turned up. Another feral, it was intended she live 'free', while under Janet's supervision, as a neutered, vaccinated feral in her grounds, with another cat that she had been found with.

They lived in Janet's garage at first, but after three weeks, they both disappeared. After five weeks, Janet spotted Diana watching her from a distance, and the cat eventually came closer to the house for her food. Over the course of three months, Diana was clearly happy being around the family, and the food bowl eventually moved into the utility area.

Perfect pet

From there, Diana transformed into a no-nonsense, easy-going pet. "She's now 14 years old and is the laziest cat you've ever known in your life!" laughs Janet. Diana ambles out into the garden, finds a sunny spot, and sleeps most of the time. And she loves human attention, too.

"It took about a year before we could pick her up, but after that we could do anything with her. She's not even scared of the vacuum cleaner; nothing fazes her at all!"

With time, Hattie and Diana have become good friends.

MEETING THE FAMILY

People and puss

Once the cat is confident in his room, then you can start to introduce him to the rest of the family, initially one at a time, so as not to overwhelm him. Each person should sit on the floor, a few feet away from the cat, and speak to him quietly, encouraging him to come and say hello.

If you hold out your hand to a cat, palm facing upwards, and rub the tip of your thumb against your forefingers, most cats magically appear to have a sniff. Gently stroke him, and spend some time with him, and then leave him for a while before introducing the next person in the family. Try not to overwhelm him.

If the cat is nervous and hiding away, don't try and force him out, but give him time to become more confident and venture out himself. This can be encouraged over time with the use of food treats, such as chicken or prawns.

If you set some basic ground rules, children and cats will get along fine.
Photo: Valerie Lewis

Child's play

Cats and kids can be great friends, but children should be taught how to behave around their new friend. Show them how to stroke the cat gently on the back of his head and along his back, and discourage any attempts to hold puss's tail or to stroke his face (having a clumsy toddler's hand come towards your face can be intimidating).

Set some basic rules: always to be gentle and calm around the cat (no racing-car games or running about when he's nearby); to leave him undisturbed when he's asleep and eating; not to tease him with food, and to leave his litter tray well alone! The allocated cat room should also be out of bounds to start with.

Keep the cat's worming up to date (see page 129), and get into the habit of all family members washing their hands regularly after cat cuddles. Obviously, never leave a cat unsupervised with young children – not just for the kids' safety, but for the cat's. Just one accident or moment of clumsiness on the child's part can ruin a budding relationship.

Fellow felines

Cats are an interesting species, because they can be very sociable with each other, but this sociability only occurs in particular circumstances. Cats may live in very friendly groups with other cats that they know well, particularly if they have 'grown up' together, but will feel very threatened by the presence of unfamiliar cats. Cats are very territorial in this way, because in their past they had to defend their patch from other cats in order to find enough food to eat. So, when you bring a new cat into a household, it is a traumatic situation both for your resident cat(s), and the new cat, who is 'landing' right in the middle of another cat's area.

Introducing a new cat has to be done very slowly and carefully – if not things can go badly wrong.

Sadly, the arrival of a new baby still results in family cats being ousted unnecessarily from the family home. But far from being a danger to a baby, a cat can boost a child's health, education and personal development...

When you're pregnant, the world and his wife suddenly believe they can proffer advice about all aspects of your life. One recurring theme, from non-pet-owning ancient relatives and in-laws, was about my beloved Cats Protection cats, Schuey and Bonnie.

It's incredible how old wives' tales still abound about cats smothering babies in cots. That, and dire warnings about worms, toxoplasmosis and any number of other hazards just made me laugh. But then I've been lucky enough to research how pets can actually benefit children, not harm them. For other parents, who haven't had access to this information, such 'advice' could well have been very confusing and stressful, and it is no wonder that some parents, faced with such anti-cat propaganda, feel pressurised into rehoming their poor puss.

Living together

Making sure that cats and baby all live safely and happily together is really just a matter of common sense – ensuring

Schuey: She took Katie's arrival in her stride.

Bonnie: After a nervous start, she learnt that the new baby would not harm her.

that the cat is wormed regularly; that the baby is never left unsupervised with a cat; that the cat is prevented from getting into the baby's cot, pram, Moses basket, etc; that the child's hands are washed after contact; that the baby is taught from a young age to respect the puss – to stroke gently, not to grab or pull, and to let sleeping cats lie.

Schuey, my Siamese cross, was nearly 11 years old when I fell pregnant with my daughter, Katie. My other puss, semi-longhaired moggie Bonnie, was nearly six. I had few concerns about how

Schu would take to a baby, as she was so bomb-proof with everyone and everything – nothing fazed her in the least. But Bonnie was something of a nervous soul with new situations.

In preparation

Almost as soon as I knew I was pregnant, I started preparing the cats for the new arrival. The nursery became out of bounds. The door was closed, and, within a week, they stopped asking to go inside that room. Whenever I bought a new piece of baby equipment, such as a buggy, the cats were introduced to it. They'd sniff it, get used to seeing me push it around, and then ignore it.

Mindful of the fact that a new baby would be something of an upheaval to their quiet, sedate lives, I decided to move their litter trays and bowls before the baby arrived. Too much change in one go could contribute to their stress, and although I knew it would be several months before the baby could crawl, I thought it preferable to get the cats used to sleeping, eating and toileting somewhere new (out of a baby and toddler's reach) before Katie arrived.

Taking maternity leave before the baby's arrival was Schu's idea of heaven. Now I was home all day, she felt it her job to sit on my 'lap' as much as possible, but I discouraged this. She was becoming quite clingy, and I knew that she would resent the sudden change when the baby was born, when I could not laze around all the time, petting and fussing her. She had a few good cuddles through the day, but I encouraged her to be independent, too.

When Katie was brought home, the cats were bemused. Their curiosity was intense and they queued up to sniff the bundle in my arms. Initially, Bonnie thought I'd brought home the devil incarnate, and hid, peeping out from behind the furniture at the strange, noisy creature I was holding. But, after a few brave sniffs, and with lots of gentle reassurance from me, she

Katie and Sam.

realised that the baby couldn't chase her and so Bonnie felt safe.

Bonnie's one sanctuary in the house, where she would retreat and feel safe whatever the circumstances, was my bed. Even if the baby were on the bed with me, Bonnie felt secure, and would settle herself just a foot from Katie.

Loving the fuss

I made sure the cats received lots of love and affection every day, and encouraged visitors to fuss them, too, and they were incredibly tolerant of the squawking little creature that had invaded their homes.

As their confidence grew, so Katie grew, and she was instantly fascinated by the cats. She said "Schu" before she said "Mummy" or any other word – something of which I was immensely proud!

Now two years old, Katie adores the cats (who have grown in number to four – with Roxy and Sammy now joining our home); she loves to help feed them; she talks to them in a 'cat voice', asking if they are okay; she knows little tricks of how to get them to come to her (by rubbing her index and middle finger against her thumb); and plays with them, too, throwing their toy mice for them to retrieve. She strokes them gently and simply adores them.

Empathy

I know that her immune system will be stronger from sharing a home with cats; I know that pet-owning children have fewer days off sick from school; I know that pet-owning children have greater empathy and respect for others; but, above all, I know that Katie's childhood, surrounded by cats, will be far happier than one devoid of pets. Seeing her gabble away to Schuey, Bonnie, Roxy or Sam, as if they are long-lost pals, I only wish that every child were as lucky to share their early years with such special feline friends.

For more information, contact Cats Protection's helpline on 08702 099 099.

GREEN-EYED MONSTER

Whatever pets you have, don't forget to pay them extra attention once the new cat comes along. It's easy to get wrapped up in the new puss, and accidentally to ignore your other animals, so make an effort to ensure they don't feel overlooked or neglected. They will accept the new cat quicker if they don't feel threatened by him or believe they need to compete for attention.

Most reputable rescue centres, such as Cats Protection, will provide a detailed leaflet or programme of introduction – read this very carefully before you take your cat home and make sure that you adhere to the advice given.

Essentially you need to start your new cat off in a separate room from your other cat(s) – preferably this room should not be an area that was used a lot by these cats. To start with the cats should not meet at all, but their scent 'swapped', by changing over food bowls, toys and bedding. Getting used to the smell of another cat is an important first step in acceptance. Once the smell of each cat is accepted by the other, visual contact can start – but again this should be gradual. For example, the cats could be fed at opposite ends of a long corridor initially, and then moved apart again when they are finished. Over time the amount of contact can be built up until the cats can happily accept being in the same area. Generally, the slower, and more carefully this process is done, the more successful it is, so try and err on the side of caution.

You will find that in most circumstances, with a little patience and time, cats will get along with other cats quite happily – and some will really love the company of another puss. Two youngsters of a similar age will play for hours and hours, leaving any older cats to snooze the day away undisturbed, joining in briefly if seized by a playful streak.

Canine chums

According to popular cartoons, cats and dogs are sworn enemies, but in reality most can cohabit quite happily – and some even become good friends.

If you have a dog at home, it's important to make sure he is cat-safe before even thinking of getting a puss. Assess how he reacts to any cats that visit your garden. Most dogs will show an interest, and will want to chase them or 'play', but some dogs can be obsessive – stiffening and shaking with excitement, drooling, stalking/hunting the cat, and so on. Terrier and sighthound breeds are more prone to this type of behaviour, given what they were originally bred for – to hunt small, furry creatures! Most breeds or types of dog can be trained not to react to a cat in the household given

enough time and patience – but this will take more time and patience for some than others!

If you are not sure about your dog's temperament, then discuss this with the rescue centre staff. Most organisations have dog-proof cats on site that they can introduce prospective owners' dogs to under safe, controlled conditions. The staff will assess the dog's reactions, and make a decision accordingly.

Most dogs do learn to accept a cat, and can make a distinction between their 'own' family cat, who will be treated with respect, and any other cats that visit their gardens, who will be chased away with vigour! Even with the most placid dog, however, great care must be taken when introducing the two pets, to ensure their safety and happiness.

The most important thing is to prevent puss from running. If he runs, the dog will chase – and it will become a great game for him (and one he will want

Good relations can be established – as long as introductions are supervised, and your dog is sound in temperament.

Photo: Maureen Pearson

to repeat). So keep all introductions calm and controlled, and don't be hasty – only move on to the next stage when puss is ready.

- Keep the new puss in his cat room, away from other pets until he is settled and is behaving confidently in there.
- To introduce the dog and cat, the dog should initially be restrained in some way – either on a leash, or in a pen (providing that they are already pen trained). Using a lead is preferable, as it is easier to sit with the dog and reward it for calm behaviour. The cat should not be restrained, and should be provided with a high shelf in the room to make him feel

more secure. The dog should be rewarded with calm praise and treats (or through the use of a 'clicker' if you are familiar with this technique) all the time that his attention is off the cat.

- Repeat these controlled introductions several times a day, just for five minutes at a time. Over the course of a week or so, the dog will start to learn that being calm in the presence of the cat is the most productive thing to do – and the cat will start to relax and learn that the dog is not a threat to him.

- Once the novelty has worn off, and they do not appear stressed or unhappy being in the same room as each other, then you can progress to the next stage – where the dog is let off the short lead, but still has a long line or house-line attached for safety. Continue rewarding the dog for not reacting to the cat.

- From here, it's just a matter of time before the two are living happily together. Don't be complacent, though – never leave them unsupervised, however well you think they are getting along.

- At mealtimes, feed puss in his cat room. Once he has become integrated into the house, make sure he can eat somewhere out of the dog's reach – where he can nibble away undisturbed. The same applies to the litter tray – not only because puss needs some peace when toileting, but also because some dogs like to eat the contents!

- If you are not happy with how the two pets are progressing, then seek professional help early on. Ask your vet for a recommendation to a local behaviour specialist. Alternatively contact a member of the Association of Pet Behaviour Counsellors (APBC) – telephone 01386 750743, email apbc@petbcent.demon.co.uk – or a behaviourist accredited through the Association for the Study of Animal Behaviour (ASAB).

Learning to live with one dog takes some getting used to; taking on five requires a special kind of 'cat-itude'!

When a very vocal tabby tom turned up outside the kitchen door one cold, wet December night in 2003, I thought he was trying his luck – that he had got caught in the rain on one of his jaunts and I was the first dry place he came across as a 'pit-stop'. I said hello, had a cuddle and checked him over. He was in good health and was well fed, so I was sure he wasn't a stray. I had seen him around for a week or so (chasing my other two cats, Schuey and Bonnie), but he was quite nervous if I approached him, and was keen to keep his distance. This December night, though, all nervousness had gone – he just wanted to come inside and be cuddled!

Keen not to encourage him in, in case he forgot to return to his proper home, I made sure he stayed outside. But he didn't leave. In the morning, he was under the porch, on the garden seat by the kitchen door. And he was still just as vocal. A check-up at the vet's revealed that he wasn't microchipped, and Cats Protection and other vets and charities in the area had no reports of a missing tabby. I advertised him in the newspaper as lost, but half hoped that he wouldn't be claimed.

For a week, he stayed in the open porch, with a box for a bed

Morris: The cat who came in from the cold.

(and a hot-water bottle at night!), and with food, water and numerous cuddles. It got very cold some nights – if he had had a home to go to, he wouldn't have stayed around.

Battling it out

After seven days, I was quite relieved that no one had called to claim him, as I had fallen in love with this charming little boy, now called Morris. He was so loving and cheeky – but, sadly, had only murderous intentions towards other cats. Every time he came into contact with Schuey or Bonnie, he was hell-bent on 'caticide'!

I put a crate in the kitchen/ dining room with a litter tray, bowls and bed, and he could see the other cats through the glass door through to the lounge. After a while, I thought they would get used to the sight of each other, and he would stop trying to fight them. But, sadly, he didn't. If ever he saw them, his hackles would rise, and he'd launch into full attack mode. On chance meetings, when he managed to get through to the lounge, the fur always flew!

I called Cats Protection, but the local Forest of Dean Branch in Gloucestershire was full and unable to take him, so I agreed to foster him until I – or the charity – could find a home. Cats Protection paid for him to be tested for any cat diseases that a wayward, fighting tom may have acquired, and, thankfully, he was clear. Then the charity paid for him to be neutered. Again, I thought he might calm down after a few months of being castrated, but it was not to be. Morris had learned that survival meant defending his territory against all-comers – and he was not going to change his ways.

Finding a home

When a friend, Justine, visited me, she fell in love with Morris, as everyone did. A real 'doggie person', who breeds and shows Bearded Collies, I was taken aback by how bowled over she was by him. Then came an offer of a home. I was relieved (it was stressful trying to keep the cats apart all the time), but also sad that our time had come to say goodbye. But I knew that, really, it was just au revoir – I would get regular updates on his progress and would regularly see him when visiting Justine.

I knew Morris would be fine with dogs. Having dog-sat a cat-friendly Golden Retriever, Ruby, I'd seen that Morris related to dogs better than to cats. He was initially apprehensive, but, within an hour, had stalked Ruby and, when he saw that she posed no threat, decided she was a great mate – he would rub against her, run after her on walks and initiate play in the garden. But how would Morris cope with five bouncy Beardies: 11-year-old Fabia, nine-year-old Fizz, four-year-old Fagan, two-year-old Florence and baby Faye, just a year old?

All the dogs had encountered cats before – at Justine's father's house, and at her sister's. They usually ignored the cats, with the exception of Fizz, who was transfixed. She would sit at the bottom of the stairs and stare, sometimes for hours, in the hope of catching a glimpse of one of the fascinating creatures.

At Justine's house, a stair-gate was put up, so Morris could have a dog-free zone upstairs. His bed, toys, litter tray and food/water bowls were put in the spare room, and he was given the run of the upper part of the house, only having to meet the dogs when he felt ready – he could take it at his own pace. After about a week, curiosity got the better of him and he decided to explore, leaping the stair-gate, on to the fridge freezer in the kitchen, and then sitting on the work surfaces where he could observe the dogs safely.

Contented companions: Morris and a Beardie chum.

"Morris was initially a bit reserved around the dogs," says Justine, "but this didn't stop him doing what he wanted to do and going where he wanted to go! Fizz, predictably, just stared at him, and the others didn't take much notice – individually.

Group action

When in a group, they would gee each other up and get excited, barking at him. Morris just stood his ground. He realised that he would be chased if he ran, so he didn't. If a dog jumped up at the kitchen counter where he was sitting, he would give them a swipe. This instilled some respect in the dogs, and they soon realised he wasn't that exciting.

"Morris quickly recognised the different dogs. Fagan is the only dog that sleeps upstairs. He is truly respectful of Morris. If Morris looks at him, he'll look the other way; if he's asleep on a bed and Morris jumps on, he'll get down. Morris thinks this is great, and rubs against Fagan – you can see Fagan thinking, 'Oh, God, what's he doing? Make it stop!'

"Florence is very gentle; she's interested in Morris but not in a horrible way. She'll go up and lick him, which Morris will accept.

"Fizz and Fabia have retired from the show ring now, so are at home with my husband most weekends, when I take the other dogs out and about. Morris is very relaxed around them because he sees more of them when the others aren't around. It took a few months, but Fizz stopped being obsessed by Morris, and now pretty much ignores him.

Right attitude

"Faye is very much the baby of the group. Being a year old, she's bouncier and more playful, and Morris isn't keen on this unpredictability. If Faye's around, he'll be more wary.

"Having a cat has worked out very well, but it wouldn't have been successful if I'd had a cat that was nervous. Morris has the right attitude – he thinks he owns the place, refuses to run from anything, and will stand his ground!"

SMALL ANIMALS

Cats have survived for thousands of years by hunting small animals for food – they aren't going to turn off their instincts when it comes to Mickey or Minnie the family pet mice, or Tweety the budgie, or Henry hamster.

Make sure such pets are kept well away from puss (not just behind the bars of a cage, but in a room that he can be shut out of) to avoid any fatal accidents.

Even if puss appears placid around such pets, don't be fooled! If he comes face to face with a mouse, strong killer instincts will be roused! What's more, the presence – or even the smell – of a cat, will be very distressing for your smaller pets.

There are extraordinary cases where cats make unusual friends – but never take a risk where small animals are concerned.

Photo: Jill Cook

THE FIRST NIGHT

When everyone has gone to bed, puss will probably stir; investigating his room and becoming braver now that all perceived threats have retired for the night. Don't be surprised to hear him using his scratching post or litter tray. You will probably hear all manner of strange bumps in the night as he leaps around, exploring, or playing with his toys.

Provided you have fully cat-proofed the room, leave him to it – interfering may send him scurrying for cover. By the morning, he will be more confident in his room, knowing every inch of it inside out.

This confidence will grow with every passing day. Soon, he will be acting as if he owns the place and has lived with you all his life.

STEP OUTSIDE...

Letting your cat outside for the first time can be incredibly stressful – for the owner! It's natural to worry, but cats are pretty smart and are very good at protecting themselves outside.

You should wait a minimum of three weeks before even thinking about letting your new cat or kitten outside. After this period you need to make an assessment of your individual cat. Some very confident cats will have settled well into their new home by this time. Many other cats will still be wary and nervous, and may not have even explored the whole of inside yet.

If your cat is still nervous in the house, and doesn't come when you call him, then postpone your plans for letting him out until he is calmer and confident all over the house. Err on the side of caution. It's important that you bond well and that you know he has accepted his new home before letting him loose. Otherwise, you run the risk that he may panic and bolt, perhaps to get back to his former home.

The timing of the first excursion outdoors is crucial. If

Wait until your cat has well and truly settled before you allow him to venture outside.

Photo: Cats Protection

there's a chance of thunder or fireworks, don't risk it – puss could be spooked and run off, without getting a lay of the land. If he hasn't assessed exactly where he is, and how to get back, he could be lost forever, or, worse, he could run under a car in blind panic. The introduction with the great outdoors should also be planned for before a mealtime; if he's hungry, he's more likely to want to return home.

It goes without saying that your cat should be microchipped and fully protected by his inoculations before he is let outside (see page 125).

Step-by-step

- Open the cat-flap (page 39) or back door and let him venture outside. Don't carry him – he won't be able to retrace his steps when he needs to return.
- He will probably step slowly and tentatively, taking in the surroundings and being alert to any dangers. Stay close by to give him reassurance. Once he has stopped being so in awe, and has had a little sniff around, show him a favourite treat (such as a ball of pâté or some fresh chicken), and encourage him to follow you back into the house.
- When he's inside, give him the treat, followed by his meal and lots of love.
- Go outside again later, and, over several sessions, gradually let him spend longer outside before tempting him back in.
- Initially, always leave the back door open, so he can escape into the house quickly if frightened by something. When he returns reliably, and you know that he can use the cat-flap, then you can close the back door when he's enjoying his jaunts outside.

IN A FLAP

Using a cat-flap isn't rocket science – certainly not for a creature as smart as a cat. Usually, it's just a case of unlocking the flap and then the cat will use it. If he's not sure of it initially, though, you'll have to show him what it's for.

- With your cat indoors, sit the other side of it, and call him through the flap. If he starts to nose the flap to open it, give lots of praise and encourage him even more.
- If he doesn't budge, show him a treat through the clear pane, or rustle his food bag.
- If he still refuses to come through, you'll have to enlist the aid of a helper, who can push the flap forward so puss

A clever cat will soon understand how the cat-flap works.
Photo: Cats Protection

can get to you through the flap.

- Once he's through, give him the tasty treat, and then put him back inside to try again.
- Each time, get the helper to push the flap forward less and less, so that the cat has to learn to push his head against it to get it to open.
- Eventually, he will be able to do it all by himself. If treats don't work, use a toy to tempt him through.

Photo: Mark Dare

CHAPTER FOUR

CARING FOR YOUR CAT

Like people, cats show a wide range of personality types and so all require looking after in an individual way. However, there are some needs that all cats have, including: a nutritionally balanced diet, environmental enrichment, grooming (and sun protection), and dental care. In addition, there may come a time when your cat's quality of life deteriorates and you may be faced with difficult decisions regarding euthanasia.

DIET

When you first take your rescue kitten or cat home, you should continue feeding the same food used by the rescue centre. Stress can cause digestive upsets – moving into a new home is stressful in itself, but giving the body a new food to deal with can cause unnecessary problems. If the only new things your cat has to cope with are the new home and family, he will settle more quickly. If you would like to change your cat's diet, it is advisable to wait until he has adjusted to the new environment first.

With such a large variety of commercial foods available today, it can be difficult to choose the best diet for your cat, especially when dietary needs change according to age, lifestyle and state of health.

Food types

Commercial pet food can be classified as 'complete' or 'complementary'. Complete foods are formulated to provide all the required nutrients in the correct balance so that no other food needs to be added, apart from water. Complementary foods, as the name implies, must be combined with other foods to provide a complete balance of nutrients; they are not intended to be the sole diet.

With the abundance of high-quality, nutritionally balanced diets on the market today, there really is no need to feed a cat an entirely home-made or fresh food diet, unless under specific veterinary advice. Creating a completely balanced diet for a cat is a complex matter. You would need to ensure that the correct amount of protein, fat, vitamins, minerals, and essential amino acids, such as taurine, are included in the diet. An incorrect amount or balance of nutrients may compromise your cat's health.

Cat food can be in wet (tinned) or dry form. Wet food has a softer texture and most brands contain about 90 per cent water. The main benefit of feeding tinned food is that a large proportion of a cat's daily water requirement is provided at the same time, although a bowl of fresh water should still be available. A good-quality complete wet food can provide everything a cat needs, but

If you feed a complete diet, you know your cat's full nutritional requirements will be met.

Fresh water should always be available – but cats are quite good at finding their own supply!
Photo: Cheryl Powell

because of the high water content you will need to feed more of it than a dry formulation.

Nowadays, more and more people are feeding their cats dry food. A good-quality complete dry food also provides everything a cat needs, except water, and is a practical option for many owners. Dry food is generally more economical than tinned food, it helps to keep the teeth and gums in good condition, it does not deteriorate as rapidly as tinned

food, and can be left out all day. Also, some cats with a tendency to develop diarrhoea are more stable on a dry diet. Cats that eat dry food will drink more because of its limited water content.

If you feed both dry and wet food, you need to reduce the amount of each, to avoid overfeeding.

Water

Water is an essential nutrient. Clean, fresh water should be available at all times regardless

TEN BEST FOOD TIPS

1 Never feed your cat a meat-free diet. Cats are carnivores and need specific nutrients that are found only in meat. You cannot have a vegetarian cat.

2 Feed a complete, nutritionally balanced diet appropriate to your cat's age, lifestyle and health status.

3 Ensure fresh, clean water is available at all times.

4 Make any changes in diet gradually over a period of about three to five days. Mix a little of the new food in with the current food, and gradually increase the amount of the new diet, while decreasing the amount of the old.

5 Don't give milk to your cat as a substitute for water – it is a food and may cause your cat to put on weight or may cause diarrhoea. Lactose-reduced milk that has been specifically formulated for cats is available from most supermarkets and pet shops.

6 Your cat does not need a vitamin supplement unless advised by a vet. It may cause an imbalance, which could be harmful.

7 Don't feed your cat raw meat; any meat should be thoroughly cooked.

8 Do not feed your cat liver. Many cats are very fond of it and if they eat excessive amounts to the exclusion of other food, they can develop a nutritional disorder called hypervitaminosis A.

9 You can still feed your cat dry food even if he has no teeth, because the gums harden and adapt well.

10 Don't feed your cat dog food – it does not meet the nutritional requirements of a cat and may potentially compromise his health.

of whether tinned or dry food is being fed. Cats often prefer their water in wide, shallow bowls because they don't like their whiskers touching the sides.

If it seems that your cat doesn't drink a lot, don't be concerned. If he is eating tinned food then he will get most of his water requirements directly from the food. Also, cats often drink from ponds, puddles or other unseen places.

Often cats prefer to sip running water, so if your cat

isn't drinking much from his bowl try providing him with a water fountain. You may find, though, that as your cat ages, he drinks more water than before. (Do report any significant changes in thirst to your vet.)

Treats

Cat treats are good for play, but watch the calories! Part of the daily allowance of dry food can be used as a play treat by putting it in a puzzle-feeder or scrunching some kibbles in a piece of paper.

It is best not to feed titbits of human food, but occasional treats of cooked fish or chicken are acceptable. Ensure that all meat or fish is fresh, free from bones and adequately cooked to avoid food poisoning.

Grass

Most cats and kittens will eat grass when they can get it, and cocksfoot grass (*Dactylis glomerata*) seems to be particularly favoured. It is a natural medicine and can act as

an emetic to induce the vomiting of fur balls. See also page 34.

Loss of appetite

Some cats are fussy eaters and you may have to try many different foods before finding a brand that they will eat consistently. It is always worth finding out what diet a new cat was fed before you got him.

If your cat normally eats well but suddenly stops eating, you can stimulate appetite in the following ways: try a range of foods at different times; warm the food slightly; or sit with your cat when you put the food down and encourage him to eat. You can even put some of the food on your finger and see if he licks it off, or you can dab some on to his lips.

If your cat has not eaten for 24 to 48 hours and appears unwell, he should be seen by a vet.

Life-stage feeding

It is important to follow the manufacturer's

recommendations on how much to feed and how long to feed a specific life-stage diet.

Feeding from birth

Normally there is no need to supplement a kitten's food from birth. If a healthy queen has a balanced diet when pregnant and during lactation, she will provide adequate nourishment for her kittens until they are weaned on to solid food.

However, if the litter is large, if the mother is unable to feed her young, or if the kittens are orphaned, you may have to supplement their diet or take over completely. This is a very demanding task, as young kittens require feeding every two hours. It is best to take advice on how to hand-rear kittens from your local vet.

Kittens

Kitten food is high in energy and protein, and can also be given to pregnant and nursing queens. Feeding the nursing queen a kitten formulation makes weaning easier, because the kittens can just start eating it when they are ready, usually

In the first weeks, the mother cat will provide all the nourishment needed by her kittens.
Photo: G. Haworth

After weaning, feed a diet that is specially formulated for kittens.
Photo: R. Thompson

around three to four weeks of age. A little warm water can be added to the food to make it easier for the kittens to start eating solid food. Water should be available at all times.

By the age of six to eight weeks, kittens should be eating a diet formulated for kittens and can be fully weaned. As they grow, kittens' dietary requirements increase rapidly, so be sure to consult the manufacturer's instructions on how much to feed at different ages. Normally, the recommended daily amount of

dry kitten food can be put out once a day and left so that the kitten can eat small amounts at frequent intervals. Tinned kitten food, however, should not be left out all day, as it will dry out and attract flies.

After weaning, a kitten should remain on a diet formulated for kittens until about one year old.

Adults
In terms of nutritional requirements, a cat is considered 'adult' between the ages of one to seven or eight years, depending on the food

manufacturer. Adult cats should have access to their daily ration of food at all times. This allows them to eat little and often throughout the day. However, if they are unable to self-regulate the amount they eat, divide the recommended daily amount into two portions for morning and evening feeding. Inability to self-regulate food intake is a common problem in rescue cats that have been living rough.

A neutered cat has lower energy requirements than an unneutered cat, so it is important to regularly monitor weight to prevent your cat from becoming overweight. Being overweight can make your cat more prone to certain diseases. If your cat has difficulty maintaining the correct weight, consider feeding a 'light' variety with a reduced calorie content.

Older cats

Cats are classed as 'senior' when they reach the age of around seven or eight years. As your cat ages, his dietary requirements will change. Numerous diets have now been formulated to meet these different requirements. In addition, if your cat develops a particular medical condition, a specific diet may help (see section on Special Diets).

At the first sign of any weight

As a cat gets older, he may do better on a diet that is specially formulated for veterans.
Photo: Claire Horton-Bussey

loss, excessive drinking or eating, it is important to take your cat to the vet for a check-up.

Pregnant and nursing queens

A pregnant cat and those cats nursing kittens need the same high-protein diet as a kitten, although in larger amounts. During pregnancy and while she is feeding her young, your cat should be given unlimited access to kitten food. Nursing cats will also drink more water because they are producing milk to feed their kittens.

Special diets

Some diets are designed to manage specific problems. Some of these foods are available from your vet, supermarket or pet shops but others can be obtained only from your vet. The latter are formulated for treating specific diseases and must be fed in accordance with your vet's instructions. Some of these diets can be detrimental if fed to a cat that doesn't have the disease or if they are fed for too long.

Special diets that are widely available and do not require veterinary supervision

• **Light**: These have been formulated for cats that are slightly overweight. As well as promoting weight loss, they can help to maintain an ideal weight.

• **Sensitive:** These diets are produced with alternative protein and carbohydrates, which can help with sensitive tummies or skin.

• **Hair-ball control**: This diet is very helpful for cats prone to problems with hair-balls, as it helps the hair to pass more easily through the digestive tract.

• **Dental care**: These diets help to reduce the build-up of plaque and calculus on the teeth. They are most commonly used as a preventive treatment, before dental disease has been identified.

As a result of grooming, hair-balls can be a problem – and a special diet may be a good option.

Photo: Paul Newton

Special diets that are available only from the vet (veterinary prescribed diets)

These diets are for cats with specific diseases, such as obesity, dental disease, food allergy, gastrointestinal disease, feline lower urinary tract disease (FLUTD), kidney disease, liver disease, heart disease, and diabetes. Other veterinary prescribed diets are available for cats that are quite run-down, have had major surgery or need extra nutritional support to help with recovery and healing.

- **Obesity:** Special diets have been developed for cats that need to lose a significant amount of weight. Managing this type of weight loss must be done in a controlled manner and needs to be regularly monitored by your veterinary practice. Overweight cats must lose weight gradually; if weight loss occurs too quickly, other medical problems may develop. Once the excess weight is lost, the vet may recommend a light (non-prescribed) diet of the kind described earlier for maintenance.

- **Dental disease**: When plaque, calculus or early periodontal disease is detected, your vet may recommend a special diet. Often the teeth are also cleaned under general anaesthetic to remove harmful accumulations.

- **Food allergy or intolerance:** These diets are useful in identifying what component(s) of food a cat is allergic to and can be used to manage the condition. Once the allergenic food item has been identified, a special diet that doesn't contain the offending agent (yet is still nutritionally balanced) can be fed.

- **Gastrointestinal disease:** Many diseases can affect the digestive system and cause vomiting, diarrhoea and/or constipation. A veterinary prescribed diet can be extremely helpful in controlling these signs, in both the short- and long-term.

- **Feline Lower Urinary Tract Disease:** FLUTD may be caused by the formation of uroliths (stones) and/or crystals in the urine, or it may have no known cause. Special diets treat crystals by making them dissolve in the urine. These diets also help prevent a recurrence of FLUTD.

- **Kidney disease:** If kidney disease is diagnosed early, a special diet can significantly slow its progression by reducing the build-up of toxins in the bloodstream and reducing the workload on the kidney.

- **Liver disease:** When the liver is not functioning properly, toxins can build up in the bloodstream and cause neurological signs. Liver disease diets aim to reduce workload on the liver, reduce toxin build-up, and help repair the damage to the liver.

- **Heart disease:** Sometimes special diets are recommended for the management of heart disease. Their main benefit is to improve blood flow, limit fluid build-up and, if necessary, help control blood pressure.

- **Diabetes:** Dietary management is a key element in treating diabetes in cats. A special diet can help maintain a consistent level of glucose in the bloodstream and improve insulin function. Diabetic cats are often not the ideal weight (they can be either overweight or underweight) and the special diet will also help rectify this.

ENVIRONMENTAL ENRICHMENT

Sleep

Cats are great conservers of energy and spend about two-thirds of their lives asleep. A basket or cardboard box, raised from the floor to exclude draughts and lined with a blanket, makes a comfortable bed. Often, however, cats choose to sleep elsewhere, such as on chairs or beds.

Exercise and play

All cats need exercise and play stimulation. A scratching post is a good investment. Buy or make a post that is tall enough to allow your cat to stretch fully, sturdy enough for him to really lean into, and with a vertical thread to enable him to work his claws down it.

A log or scratching board can also help your cat keep his claws sharpened. Scratching and stretching enable your cat to flex his muscles and shed old claw sheaths, and he's less likely to scratch the furniture!

Toys also help to keep cats active. Table tennis balls and empty cotton reels are enjoyed just as much as catnip mice and purpose-made toys. Of course, toys burst into life when you play with your cat. Flicking a cotton reel across the floor, or pulling a toy attached to the end of a string, will soon get your cat on his feet and ready to chase.

A couple of play sessions a day will keep your cat mentally stimulated, and will be a good stress-reliever for you too – playing with a cat is very therapeutic!

All cats need exercise, as well as mental stimulation.
Photo: Michelle Holden

INDOOR CATS

Cats vary in how well they adapt to becoming indoor cats. For example, older cats that love to snooze are more likely to adapt well than a cat that is used to going out, particularly one that is used to maintaining a large territory size. However, most young adult cats just love the great outdoors and it would be wrong to confine them inside. Your rescue centre will match the right cat to you; if you want a house-cat, discuss this when you visit the rescue facility.

Fresh air and sunshine are necessary for us all, so if your cat is confined to a flat without a safe, enclosed balcony, fit a wire frame to one window that will admit air and sunshine but prevent the risk of falling from a height. It is unsafe to allow cats out on to narrow ledges or open roofs. Many animals are killed or severely injured every year by lunging at a bird or butterfly and missing their

Provided with a stimulating environment, a cat is content to live indoors.
Photo: Betty Chadwick

footing. It is not true that a cat will always land on his feet – even if he does, he will likely be injured by the fall.

It is especially important to provide extra mental and physical stimulation for indoor-living cats. Your home is the cat's entire world – he will need to climb, stretch, scratch, stalk toys and play-hunt all within the confines of your house. Some people set aside a cat room, adapted as a play room. If carpeting the walls and setting up tunnels and walkways in a spare room is out of the question, there are many other ways of providing exercise. Providing access to three dimension space is a must – this can be through a cat tree, or by providing shelves at different heights, that might, for example, allow a cat up to the top of a book case or kitchen unit.

A good variety of toys is also important. Toys that your cat can play with alone should ideally be changed regularly, so they are novel, and it is best if they are moving toys that attract his attention. Playing with your cat, providing lots of options for different activities, and encouraging him to use his mind and body, will prevent him from becoming frustrated.

OLDER CATS

Older cats are wonderful! Generally quieter and more sensible than younger cats or kittens, they are often used to household life, and know the ground rules of living with people. More placid, the older cat is more likely to enjoy long lap cuddles than a youngster and can be an excellent companion. If you enjoy pampering a cat, an older one is much more likely to appreciate the attention than a kitten would.

However, it is important to remember that even old cats are all individuals, and some may appreciate close contact and cuddles more than others. It is still important to ask rescue centre staff to find an older cat for you that is most suited to your needs and expectations.

Older cats are often less supple, so they may need extra help with grooming. Very long-haired cats can get messy around their rear ends. Some owners like to trim the fur carefully under the tail to stop faeces and cat litter from sticking there. The area may need cleaning with a pet wipe or damp flannel, and the hair should be combed very carefully.

Many older cats love their home comforts, so attention should also be paid to their sleeping habits. They will spend more time sleeping as they advance in years, and will need a cosy, warm, draught-free place. At night, or in cold weather, an older cat may appreciate a heated pet pad in the bedding, or a warm (not hot), covered hot-water bottle.

The type of bed you provide may need changing, too, depending on its size and shape. Most elderly cats find it difficult to curl up into a ball as they once did, and so a larger bed may be necessary. Also,

An older cat will enjoy quality time with his family.
Photo: Wendy Mitchell

depleted fat stores usually lead to boniness, so fleecy veterinary-type bedding or a similarly thick, comfortable bedding should be used. Beanbags can be good, provided they are not so deep that the cat has difficulty getting out of them.

Some older cats become disorientated when they wake, and will call out. This behaviour can be a sign of a medical disease, such as hyper-thyroidism, or cognitive dysfunction, so you should first take your cat to the vet for a check-up. If no medical cause is found for the change in behaviour, placing your cat's bed in your bedroom will help you to monitor this and provide comfort if needed.

Make sure that your oldie is able to get in and out of his litter tray easily too – a shallow-sided tray is a good idea to prevent accidents happening.

It is recommended that older cats be examined by a vet every six months. Because senior cats are more likely to develop age-related diseases, the earlier these are detected, the better the chance of treating and managing

A *mature approach to life has many benefits, as Joan Rookledge – and other owners of the older mog – are well aware.*

Joan and husband Peter, from Selsey, West Sussex, have had cats all their lives – from kittens through to golden oldies. When they heard that their local Cats Protection Branch had an older cat that was being overlooked in favour of kittens and other young cats, they decided to offer her a home.

Twelve-year-old Jessie had been at Cats Protection's Chichester, Bognor Regis & District Branch for around five weeks, and although Joan had sworn never to have another cat again, she soon changed her mind when she heard of Jessie's plight.

"I'd lost my cat Sydney about six weeks before," explains Joan. "He was a dear old cat – a real character. I got him from Cats Protection when he was 15 years, and had him for nine

Jessie: Given a chance to live out her days in comfort.

months before he became ill and had to be put to sleep. After Sydney, I was very upset and I said "I'm not having any more" but a few weeks passed and when I heard about Jessie from a friend who is a volunteer at the Branch, it seemed such a pity that she needed a home and we had a home to give."

Home comforts

Jessie, like many older cats, loved her home comforts, and was not thriving in being in a pen. She had been the much-loved pet of an elderly couple who had to give her up for adoption when they went into a retirement home that did not allow pets. Fortunately, Joan was happy to offer a lap and some home comforts to help Jessie through her sadness.

"She's not a cat I would have usually chosen: she was so overweight – a real lump – but she has a lovely character and has settled in so well. When we go away for a few days, I arrange for a friend to come and look after Jessie, and when we return, you can tell that she's really missed us.

"The main benefit of an older cat is that they tend to stay closer to home. Jessie wanders out to the fenced garden and doesn't go anywhere else, so I don't worry where she is, as I did with younger cats," says Joan.

Fortunately, Jessie is in very good health, and is very sprightly at 14 years. "She had a good MOT before she came to me," explains Joan, "although she is still overweight! It's taking a while to get the excess pounds off her from when she was overly pampered in her previous home."

Favouring oldies

As for the future, Joan admits that she probably would take on another oldie. "They just want a comfortable bed and a peaceful existence," she says, "and they can be very long-lived. One of my former cats, Weenie, was 24 years old when she died!"

them successfully. If you notice any change in your older cat's behaviour, his eating, drinking and toileting habits, seek veterinary advice without delay.

NIGHT CURFEW

For a cat's safety, and for your own peace of mind, it is best that your cat is kept in overnight. Many road accidents involving cats take place during the hours of darkness when cats are less visible to drivers.

GROOMING

Cats are fastidious groomers and generally keep their coats very clean. However, sometimes they need a helping hand from us. Grooming your cat daily is especially good for long-haired breeds. Brushing and combing removes loose hair, dirt and dust. Grooming also helps to prevent hair-balls because the cat ingests less hair.

Grooming your cat has another important benefit – it is

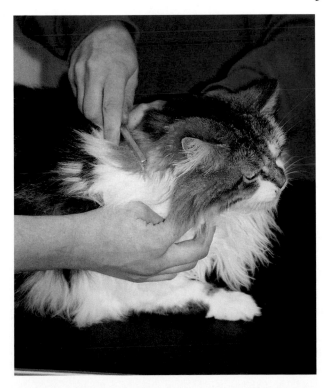

If you have a long-haired cat, you may need extra help to hold the cat while you groom.

a good reason to spend time with puss. Setting aside time every day, devoted exclusively to your cat, can be relaxing in today's frantically paced life.

The type of comb or brush you need will depend on the thickness of your cat's coat. Your rescue centre can recommend an appropriate grooming tool.

If your cat stops grooming or if his coat changes, he may be unwell and should be examined by a vet.

DENTAL CARE

Many adult cats develop a heavy build-up of plaque and tartar (also known as calculus) on their teeth, which causes great discomfort when eating and will eventually lead to a refusal to eat and the loss of teeth. A vet can remove the material while the cat is under a general anaesthetic. See the section on dental disease in Chapter Six.

One of the best things you can do at home to prevent or reduce excessive plaque and tartar formation is to brush the cat's teeth. Daily brushing is ideal, but this is often not practical, so brush as often as you can manage. You can buy a finger brush or a pet toothbrush from your vet or pet store, or you can use a small toothbrush intended for babies. Special toothpastes have been formulated for use on cats. Never use toothpaste intended for humans, as it contains ingredients that your cat should not swallow.

Brushing a cat's teeth is not the easiest job in the world, but most cats get used to it, particularly if you start when they are young. With a cat not used to the procedure, it is best to introduce it gradually: First, stroke around the face and mouth with the finger brush on the end of your finger. Then, another time, gently put the finger brush into the side of the mouth and rub the teeth gently. Keep these initial dental sessions short, and increase gradually.

If brushing isn't tolerated,

It is important to keep teeth and gums clean and healthy.
Photo: Gwen Conway

special pastes with enzymes that reduce plaque formation can be purchased from the vet. These are simply put on the cat's paws or in his mouth.

The use of dry diets or special cat chews will also help decrease plaque and tartar formation. Also, refer to the section on diet for more information on food formulated specially for dealing with dental care and disease.

SUN CARE

White cats, or those with sparse hair, are particularly prone to skin cancer, especially on the ears and nose. If the cancer occurs on the ears, it can be treated by surgically removing the tips of the ears.

If you have a white cat (or one with areas of skin that have little hair covering) that likes to bask in the sun you can apply UVA/UVB sunscreen to the nose, ears and other exposed areas. Another preventive measure is to keep susceptible cats indoors when the sun is at its hottest (between 10am and 3pm). The more hours a cat spends in the sun unprotected by sunscreen, the more likely he is to develop skin cancer.

EUTHANASIA

There may come a time when your cat will begin to suffer through illness or old age. If this happens, it is kinder to end the pain and have him put to sleep.

Meaning 'gentle death', euthanasia is the technical term for putting an animal to sleep. An anaesthetic overdose is usually injected into the vein of a foreleg, sending the cat into a deep sleep and then stopping the heart.

This is never an easy decision to make, especially if you have been companions for many years. Understandably, you will want to delay making the decision for as long as possible, but you do need to consider the quality of your cat's life. An illness may be treatable for a while, but eventually your cat may begin to show signs of distress. Your vet is best placed to advise you on the most suitable course of action. Some questions to think about and discuss with the vet are:

- Has your cat stopped or significantly reduced his normal day-to-day activities?
- Does he interact with you as much as usual or has he become quiet, spending much more of his time sleeping in a place away from noise and people?
- Is your cat in continual pain or discomfort?
- Are drugs no longer effective?
- Is treatment no longer possible?
- If injured, what is the likelihood of recovery?
- Does your cat have an incurable age- or illness-related condition?

Sometimes it's possible to delay euthanasia for a day, so you can say goodbye the way

Sometimes you will need to make a judgement about your cat's quality of life.
Photo: Julie Suffolk

you wish. Share your last night together pampering your cat with love and his favourite foods. Of course, if your cat is suffering, it's best not to prolong the pain. You can arrange for your vet to euthanase your cat at home. This is often less stressful for everyone.

The vet will ask you whether you would prefer your cat to be buried or cremated. If you would like the ashes returned, your cat can be individually cremated and the ashes returned to you in a scatter box, urn or casket. Unless local bylaws forbid it, burial can take place in your garden. In some areas, you may be able to take your cat's body to a pet cemetery or pet crematorium. Your vet will be able to advise you.

Dealing with loss

In an ideal world, cats would live as long as humans, but sadly this isn't the case. A likely lifespan for a healthy cat is about 15 years, but some do live longer.

The most we can wish for is that our cats will die peacefully in their sleep after a long and happy life. But sometimes they

In time, you will be able to look back on all the happy moments you shared with your cat.

Photo: Sue Westerman

die prematurely through illness or accident. If your cat dies unexpectedly or in an accident, your grief can be made worse by feelings of anger or guilt. Rather than blaming yourself for an accident you couldn't have prevented, think of the good times you spent together and try not to feel guilty. Cats are notoriously curious, so no matter how much you want to ensure your pet's safety, sometimes accidents just can't be avoided.

If your cat dies suddenly for no apparent reason, you can request a post mortem. It may have been in an accident that left no external damage but that caused internal injuries. He could have died from heart failure, a stroke or from an illness that revealed no signs. Occasionally, cats die of no known medical cause.

The sense of loss you feel if a cat goes missing can be just as hard to cope with. Letting go can be even more difficult, as there's no body to serve as a focal point for your grief. You are left wondering about what has become of your pet and there is always the hope that the cat may return one day. Many cats get lost but do eventually find a new home.

For you, it may be important to say goodbye in your own way. Holding a memorial service to commemorate your cat may help you bid farewell. In place of your cat's body, you can bury his favourite toys or you can put an obituary in a cat magazine. You can even have a memorial plaque made, or plant a rose bush in your cat's memory.

Losing your beloved pet can be as traumatic as the death of any other family member. Guilt, grief and anger are natural reactions and you will need time to come to terms with your loss. Try to seek consolation by remembering the joy your cat brought you. If your cat was put to sleep, take comfort in the fact that your loving act of mercy has spared your cat from any further suffering.

There are many avenues of help open to you when you lose your pet. A pet bereavement helpline (0800 096 6606) is run jointly by the Society for Companion Animal Studies (SCAS) and The Blue Cross. The first call is free, and you'll be referred to a 'telephone befriender' in your area who, having experienced the death of his or her own pet, will understand what you are going through and be able to offer you the support you need.

Books are another source of help. *Absent Friend* by Laura and Martyn Lee, and *Goodbye Dear Friend* by Virginia Ironside are recommended, but see your local bookshop for the many other titles that offer practical and emotional support.

There are some children's books, too, which help to explain the death of a pet to youngsters. For websites devoted to pet loss, most search engines will produce many, many leads.

Photo: Roland Woodhall

CHAPTER FIVE

SOCIALISATION AND CAT BEHAVIOUR

I f a cat is to be a confident, happy pet in the domestic home, he must be well socialised when young. The socialisation phase of a kitten's development lasts from approximately two weeks of age, tapering off from seven or eight weeks, although there is some variation between individual kittens.

During this phase, kittens will accept all the things that they come across as a 'normal' part of their world. They learn that all the people, other animals, sights, smells and sounds that they come across during this period are a normal part of life, and will be more likely to

accept them as they become adults. Conversely, they are much more likely to be scared of anything that they don't come across during this period once they become adults. It's therefore crucial that young kittens meet as many different people as possible.

All new experiences – whether with people, the vacuum cleaner, the family dog, the vet – should be positive: the cat should find them enjoyable, so give rewards, cuddles, games and verbal praise to keep his confidence up, and to help him view novel items and experiences as fun.

After the socialisation period,

kittens will be fearful of new things that they come across. So, a kitten that first comes into contact with, for example, children when he is 12 weeks old may be very scared, and needs to be taught – gradually and carefully, with time and patience – that children are nice. Equally, adult cats that are fearful of people should be allowed to approach you in their own time – it will be counterproductive to force contact, as you will only make them feel more scared of you.

HOUSE MANNERS

AGGRESSION TOWARDS PEOPLE

Aggression can occur in cats for a number of reasons – commonly, it occurs in cats that are fearful of people and anxious about being approached or handled. The cat learns that aggression is an effective way of getting people to let go of them – it usually works! Because the cat is scared, getting away is very rewarding, and means that the

A kitten needs to learn through positive experiences.
Photo: Mark Tarratt

cat will learn to show aggression again next time someone approaches. This type of aggression most often (but not exclusively) occurs when the cat is approached by someone.

The other common reason for cats showing aggression towards people is where they learn, as kittens and young cats, that this is a good way of interacting with people. In their natural environment, kittens start to play as a way of 'practising' hunting behaviours. To begin with, this is directed at all sorts of objects, but, as they develop, their mothers direct the kittens' behaviour towards appropriate prey items.

In the home environment, people often make the mistake of playing with kittens with their fingers – or by moving their feet around under the duvet. Although this is great fun with a young kitten, it can start to direct play/predatory behaviours towards bits of you, which isn't such fun with an adult cat!

Often this type of aggression appears as 'ambushing' where the cat lies in wait, ready to attack as soon as you walk by. Cats showing this type of behaviour often don't have many other things to do in their environment.

Make sure that your cat has lots of appropriate objects to attack – there are hundreds of good toys available. Spend time playing with your cat, but make sure the games are distant from the body (for example, using 'fishing rod' type toys).

When a cat does attack you, it is best to remain completely still. This may seem difficult to do, but any movement will stimulate him to bite or scratch more (as this is what he would do with a 'natural' prey item). If you stay still, you will find that he loses interest quickly, at which point you can move away. If possible, wear thick clothes (trousers or gloves, depending on where the attacks occur) to make it easier for you to remain still.

If you have a cat that is persistently showing aggression to you, it is important that you take him to your vet first. There are a number of medical conditions that can cause aggression, and your vet will need to test for these. If no medical cause is found, ask your vet to refer you to a suitably qualified behaviour specialist (see page 115).

HOUSE-SOILING

House-soiling can occur in different forms – it can be due to toileting problems (either urine or faeces), or can be related to urine spraying for scent marking. It is important to realise that urine spraying and urination for toileting reasons are completely different behaviours, and cats will show these behaviours for different reasons.

Toileting

When a cat urinates to go to the toilet, he will squat down and pass a fairly large volume of liquid on a horizontal surface. This behaviour is, just as it is for us, a way of getting rid of waste products from the body, and cats will prefer to find a quiet, secluded location with a suitable material for burying.

Once they have an established toileting site, cats don't suddenly change their toileting habits for no reason. So, if your cat starts to toilet away from the litter tray, or stops going outside to toilet, you need to consider why it is that the litter tray is no longer acceptable for him (see pages 42 and 109).

Check out relations between other cats – this can be a source of stress.
Photo: Carolyn Chase

Urine spraying

Unlike toileting, spraying is carried out with the cat standing up and pumping out small jets of urine on to a vertical surface.

Spraying is a behaviour rather like facial marking for the cat – it is a way of leaving a scent mark in his environment. In unneutered cats, it is used to attract members of the opposite sex, but it also occurs in neutered cats of both sexes. Whereas facial marking is used where cats feel relaxed and happy in their environment, cats will use the urine spray scent to indicate those parts of their territory where they feel anxious or insecure. In most cases, this will be where there is an overlap over territory between neighbouring cats (or between cats in the same household) that don't see each other as part of the same social group. The spray mark is like a 'warning message' to the resident cat to be careful in that part of their patch. Because it is a message, it makes sense for the cat to check up on his marks, topping them up if they have faded.

The kinds of situations where cats may start to spray are:

• *The cat is living with too many other cats in close quarters*
Think hard about the number of cats you keep. Too many cats in too small an area can often be highly stressful for the animals, and they will seek to carve out their own bit of personal space. Providing each cat with his own 'core area', where his food, water, litter tray and toys are kept, will help reduce the amount of conflict in a household, as cats will need to pass each other less in order to get the things that they need.

   If only one of the cats in a household is a sprayer, then he may benefit from a less crowded living environment in another home, or a 'patch' that is just his.

• *The cat feeling threatened by neighbouring cats.*
A neighbour's cat coming in – or peering in – through the cat-flap can intimidate a moggie. As before, your cat should be given his own safe spot (with his food, water, litter tray and toys) in the house, totally undisturbed, to which he can retreat when under pressure. If the cat-flap is the source of stress, lock it when you are not around, to ensure that 'foreign' cats cannot come in, or you can dispense with it altogether.

• *Other changes in the house are causing insecurity*
Cats can also start to spray for other reasons – for example, at the arrival of visitors, a new baby, builders, or even a new scent entering the house on your feet. Sometimes cats are disturbed by changes in their owner's routine or behaviour.

• *Attention seeking*
Occasionally, cats can learn

If you see a marked change in behaviour – such as the resident cats failing to get on with each other – you will need to find the underlying cause.

Photo: Betty Chadwick

that spraying is an effective way of getting people to jump up and be exciting! This is particularly the case with oriental breeds of cat, but can also happen with moggies. In these cases the spraying usually starts for other reasons, but the cat learns over time to use the behaviour to get people going!

If your cat has suddenly taken to spraying in inappropriate places around the home, the first step is to take him to the vet for a health check. This is particularly important if you know that nothing new or potentially stressful (such as the arrival of other cats in the neighbourhood, etc) in your cat's immediate environment could be responsible for the change in behaviour.

A vet will be able to investigate whether there's a medical reason for the spraying. If no medical cause is found, your vet will be able to refer you to a qualified behaviour specialist (see page 115).

In the treatment of urine spraying, it is essential to

Some cats are more sensitive than others; it will help if you understand what triggers a particular pattern of behaviour.

Photo: Carole Valentine

identify the reason that puss is spraying and deal with this. In addition, it is important to stop him 'topping up' existing marks as he patrols around. To do this you can:

• Clean the area thoroughly. Most popular household cleaners are unsuitable, as they contain ammonia and chlorine. Both of these compounds are found in cat urine, so you can actually make the problem worse! Wash any soiled areas with a warm, dilute solution of biological washing powder, which removes the protein components in your cat's urine.

• Rinse the area with cold water and allow to dry.

• Next, spray or dab the whole area with surgical spirit and leave to dry thoroughly.

- Some specialist products are specifically designed for cleaning up accidents. Your pet shop or vet will have details.
- Whatever you use, remember always to do a small patch test on any material first to ensure that it will not be damaged.
- Do not allow your cat access to rooms or the area where you are undertaking this cleaning regime. In fact, it's a good idea to restrict access for a couple of days.

The use of commercially available synthetic pheromones has been found to be effective, in combination with behaviour therapy to resolve the reason for spraying. These products discourage the cat from 'topping up' previously sprayed areas by changing his perception of the area from one associated with anxiety, to one associated with comfort. Obviously, this will only be effective if the cause of anxiety is dealt with at the same time!

Finally, it's important never to get angry and punish your cat for spraying. Not only is it unkind but it's also counterproductive. You will simply make your cat more stressed, anxious and insecure – meaning he will be even more likely to spray in an attempt to relieve such feelings.

SCRATCHING

Cats need to scratch to remove old claw husks. It's also an important part of their stretching ritual – they will stretch up high, dig their claws in and pull. If you do not provide adequate scratching opportunities, puss will have no choice but to scratch your sofa, curtains and carpets.

If you have provided a scratching post, but your cat still scratches, it's probably because the scratching post isn't as good for scratching as your sofa is! Remember that your cat can't read labels – he won't know that the funny little piece of furniture you bought is

A cat that has a full and varied life is far less likely to suffer from stress or any other behavioural problems.

Photo: Julie Pettitt

meant to be a scratching post; he will just look for the item in the room that most fulfils his needs for a scratching post. For most cats the important criteria of a scratching post are:

- Being high enough to stretch up
- Being sturdy enough to lean into
- Having a vertical thread to work claws down.

If your cat isn't using your scratch post, but uses the back of the sofa instead, then the sofa probably meets these criteria better. The answer is simple – temporarily cover the back of the sofa with thick plastic to prevent access, and provide a really suitable scratching post nearby.

Sometimes elderly cats can't cope with stretching up athletically, and may need a horizontal scratching pad.

As well as working their nails, cats will also scratch as a way of leaving a scent mark, just as they do with urine spraying and facial rubbing.

If this is the case, the location of the scratching tends to be more significant – for example, it may be near entrance or exit points, or where cats pass each other at the bottom of the stairs. If this is the case, the resolution of the problem will involve dealing with the insecurities leading to his scent marking. As with urine spraying, this will depend on the cause of insecurity, but may involve, for example, providing resources (such as food, water and litter trays) in more places around the house in a multi-cat household to reduce the need for individual cats to pass each other.

OTHER PROBLEM BEHAVIOURS

There is a range of other behaviours that cats can show in response to events in their environment that cause them stress. For example, cats can chew, or even swallow, items that are not food, such as pieces of cloth, or even plastic. Some cats may develop behaviours such as binge eating and vomiting, or excessively grooming or plucking at their hair. Many cats are fearful of specific events, such as noises, or the arrival of visitors.

If you see your cat showing any of these behaviours, or indeed if he is behaving in any other way that is not normal

for him, it is important that your first port of call is your vet. Many types of behavioural change can be precipitated by medical conditions, so it is important that these possibilities are examined first. When medical causes are ruled out, your vet will be able to refer you to a behaviour specialist.

SEEING A BEHAVIOURIST

There are lots of ideas and theories about cat behaviour – some of them have a good basis in science and research, but many do not. When seeking help for behaviour problems with your cat it is important that you take him to see somebody who is adequately trained, qualified and experienced to be able to give you appropriate advice.

Many people call themselves 'behaviourists' but they have no real qualification or training – there are now, however, organisations that promote a responsible and professional approach to behaviour therapy, and these should be your first port of call. Ask your vet to refer you to either:

- A veterinary surgeon that specialises in behaviour therapy and has a postgraduate qualification in this area.
- A clinical behaviourist who is accredited and recognised by the Association for the Study of Animal Behaviour (ASAB).
- A member of the Association of Pet Behaviour Counsellors (APBC).

For details see page 68.

FUN TRICKS

Dogs aren't the only pets that can be taught tricks. Cats are very trainable, provided they are motivated. The main difference between the two species is how easily they are motivated to do things – for example, by food or attention. Generally, a cat will concentrate on a task for less time than a dog, so training sessions need to be kept short and sweet.

The secret of training a cat is to find a reward that he really loves, such as pieces of chicken, or a prawn, or even a game. Rather than using them as a bribe, these treats are used as rewards.

SIT

For example, if you wait until your cat sits down, and then give him a prawn, he will soon learn that sitting is a good thing to do. Once he keeps coming up to you and sitting, you can add a 'cue word' ('sit' is the most obvious in this example!) just before he sits. He will then associate the word with the action – if he only gets the prawn when he sits on the cue, he will have learned to sit on 'command'.

FETCH

Another trick you can teach him is to fetch on command. Cats naturally carry things in their mouths – their prey, kittens, etc. In this exercise, the aim is to get puss to carry the toy back to you. It's a

If you can train a cat with treats, he will soon learn to focus on you.
Photo: Alan Christie

rewarding game for the cat – you throw a toy, he fetches it, and then he is rewarded when you throw the toy again for him to chase and play with.

- Sit in the middle of a room, with two toys to hand. Show one to your cat and get him interested in it (wiggle it around to get him motivated).
- Throw the toy a few feet away, and he will chase after it. He will play with it and mouth it, and, at some point, will probably pick it up in his mouth to take it to the side of the room or under a table (as he would with prey).
- As soon as he has the toy in his mouth, call him to you and show him the other toy you have. As soon as he makes a step towards you, praise him and encourage him to come.
- When he does, give him a treat, and throw the new toy for him to play with.

Brought up with Burmese, Belinda Price always knew she would have cats in her life, and assumed she would follow in her parents' footsteps and have pedigree pusses. When she married and set up a home of her own, in Ellwood, Gloucestershire, she had the good fortune to move next to Cats Protection's Forest of Dean Branch organiser, Sara Cox, who had pens in her garden. From her window, Belinda saw that two white little kittens were awaiting a home, and asked her neighbour about the bundles of fluff...

"I was told that the kittens were deaf and Cats Protection was having problems finding them a home, as they needed to be indoor cats (because of the risk of road accidents or other dangers). When I saw them, I fell in love with them. Not just because they were cute and fluffy, but because they needed a home.

"Although they are siblings, Daisy and Polo have such different personalities. Polo worships his sister, but she doesn't want anything to do with him!

Wild things

"Having spent some time in the pen, they were a little crazy at first. Sara had spent hours with them, playing and handling them, but they were rather wild still. I remember night times being the worst. I'd lie in bed, awake most of the night, listening to them thudding up and down the stairs. They make so much noise – probably because they can't hear themselves!

"One night we came back to the house to find the stereo on full-blast. It sounded as if there was a wild party in full swing. The cats were fast asleep, oblivious to it all. They had obviously been playing and had pounced on the stereo, switching it on. Then, when they had tired, they went to sleep. The

Daisy and Polo: With love and patience, they adapted to their new home.

neighbours must have wondered what was going on!

"They don't mew often, but when they do, it's really noisy, too! I'm used to Burmese, who are vocal and loud, but Daisy and Polo are louder still.

"It took them a while to settle in – lots of playing and handling and loving them, as well as giving them their space. They can still be a little nervous of people they don't know, but they are confident with us, and regular visitors, now.

"My dad built them a run at the back of the house, with a cat-flap to indoors. It's like a big rabbit hutch, all covered, so they can see outside and get fresh air without being in danger.

"Having two of them means

SMITTEN WITH KITTENS

they play a lot together and use up their energy. They really race around the house, then dive under the bed. They are probably calming down a little now they are five years old, but they are still very energetic and love their toys.

Love and attention

"People think that cats don't need as much attention as dogs, but you still need to be committed. Before bringing them home, I made sure I had prepared everything – made everywhere safe and had bought everything they needed. You should also be prepared for a few sleepless nights!

Time out

"Kittens – regardless of whether they can hear or not – need time and attention. You need to play with them, handle them, and love them. You also need to keep your wits about you – being sure to keep them indoors until they are allowed to go out. You have to remind visitors about this, and be vigilant and thoughtful.

"I don't think of Daisy and Polo as being deaf at all. Their other senses make up for their lack of hearing. For example, when I go to feed them, they'll be there, rubbing against my legs or sitting in front of the cupboard.

Rescue cats any day!

"Perhaps they sense vibrations, I don't know. They'll always appear when I come into the house, too. I talk to them as if they can hear; I can't help myself – it just comes naturally to want to speak to them!

"I'm converted now. I always knew I'd share my home with cats, but had assumed it would be with Burmese.

"Now, I jokingly tell my parents that they can keep their posh cats; I recommend giving homes to those who really need them – from Cats Protection."

- With practice, he will soon catch on to what the game is, and will come back to you with the toy. Then, you can say, "Fetch", so he learns to associate the command word with the action of retrieving a toy.

FURTHER FUN

There are lots of other tricks you can teach your cat, to spice up your play sessions together and to keep his brain ticking over. Books such as *Clicker Training For Cats* by Karen Pryor are good starting points. If you have a cat with the right 'can do' attitude, the sky's the limit as to what you can achieve. Even if you are not hugely successful, you will still have a lot of fun spending time together, cementing the special relationship between cat and owner.

Karen Pryor's book **Clicker Training For Cats.**

Photo: Betty Chadwick

CHAPTER SIX

HEALTH CARE

Generally, the health care needs of rescued cats are no different from those of any other cat. Regular health checks at the vet's (see page 45 on registering with a vet), neutering, vaccination, and regular treatment against fleas and worms are all part of a preventive health care programme for any puss.

Many rescue centres make sure that each cat has a veterinary check upon arriving at the centre to assess the cat's current state of health. Rescue centres often have cats neutered, vaccinated, and treated for fleas and worms before rehoming them. Some also microchip the cat. Also, many centres blood test cats for feline leukaemia virus (FeLV) and feline immunodeficiency virus (FIV) – see pages 134. It is worth asking what is known about a cat's medical history when you adopt.

NEUTERING

Neutering is an important part of preventive feline health care. Most rescue organisations neuter cats before rehoming, but if you adopt a very young kitten, you must agree to have it neutered and to provide evidence to the organisation

There are too many unwanted cats, so population control should always be a serious consideration.

Photo: Sue Cooper

that this has been done. There is a huge number of unwanted, stray and feral cats in the UK. Cats are prolific breeders, and a high incidence of unneutered cats results in even more, many of whom will be homeless and have a poor quality of life.

As well as population control, neutering has many health benefits for a cat. Some incurable infectious diseases, such as feline leukaemia virus (FeLV) and feline immunodeficiency virus (FIV), are transmitted via mating or fighting. These diseases in a queen can be passed on to her kittens. Cats that fight a lot (usually male) are more likely to spread infectious disease and will be more prone to injuries, such as abscesses. Neutered cats will not be involved in mating and will be less likely to fight. Female cats that are not neutered are at higher risk of infection of the womb, complications during pregnancy and kittening, and may be at higher risk of mammary cancer.

Unneutered cats behave quite differently from neutered cats. Unneutered females will 'call' about every two weeks from about January to October unless they are pregnant. This 'calling' behaviour is to attract male cats for mating.

Unneutered male cats will have a larger territorial range. They will respond to the call of the female, they will fight with other cats more, and will be more likely to spray urine (to mark territory) and may be more aggressive to people. These cats may also be at greater risk of being involved in a road traffic accident.

Consult your vet about the best time to neuter your cat. Traditionally, this is carried out at approximately six months, but more modern practice is to neuter from around four months onwards.

VACCINATION

Vaccination has significantly reduced the incidence and severity of certain feline diseases and is another essential part of responsible cat care.

Many cats in a rescue centre will have already been vaccinated, so, when taking your cat home, ask what vaccines he has had and when the next one is due.

Kittens require their first vaccine from nine weeks of age, followed by another at 12 weeks. Again, it is advisable to check if he has received any vaccines at the rescue centre.

Regular booster vaccinations throughout a cat's life are recommended to help protect him from disease. These usually take place annually, although it is best to consult your vet on the type and frequency of vaccination that is most appropriate for your cat. Many people see the booster vaccinations as a great time for your cat to have a general check-up too, to ensure he remains fit and healthy.

DISEASES WE CAN VACCINATE AGAINST

Feline infectious enteritis, feline panleucopaenia

- This devastating disease in kittens is caused by feline parvovirus (FPV). It causes death very quickly, often despite intensive treatment.

- The virus causes a severe form of gastroenteritis, often with signs of acute vomiting and diarrhoea, but, if the disease is very severe, there may be no signs other than sudden death. If a kitten is infected before or shortly after birth, the virus can cause severe brain damage.

- The virus is very hardy and can survive in the environment for over a year.

- Vaccination is extremely effective and has reduced the incidence of disease; however, outbreaks can still occur.

- Vaccination against FPV is always included as part of a vaccination programme and so is considered a 'core' vaccine.

Cat 'flu

- This is most commonly caused by feline herpes virus (FHV-1) and/or feline calicivirus (FCV).

- Common signs of 'flu include sneezing, inflamed eyes (conjunctivitis), discharge from the nose and eyes, ulcerations in the mouth, inflamed throat and coughing.

- Treatment usually involves antibiotics (to help prevent or to reduce secondary bacterial infections) and supportive care.

- Severe cases of this disease can result in lifelong recurrent bouts of illness.

- Once infected, your cat may release the virus into the environment and be infectious to other cats.

- There are many strains of calicivirus and new strains occur frequently. Vaccines do not protect against all of them, which is why 'flu is still a common disease. Despite this, vaccination does help control infection.

All cats should be vaccinated against infectious diseases.

Photo: Dai Brogden

- FHV and FCV vaccines are also 'core' vaccines.

Feline chlamydophilosis or chlamydia

- *Chlamydophila felis* is a specialised type of bacterium that causes mild to severe inflammation and discharge from one or both eyes. Sometimes sneezing and discharge from the nose occurs, and it occasionally affects people.
- The disease responds well to antibiotics, but the course of treatment for *Chlamydophila felis* can be quite long.
- It isn't a problem in all geographical areas, but, where it is a problem, vaccination has been very helpful in reducing disease incidence. This is especially so in a rescue or multi-cat environment.

Feline bordetellosis

- This disease is thought to be on the increase in cats. It is caused by a bacterial agent, *Bordetella bronchiseptica*, and is similar to kennel cough in dogs. It is usually found in association with one of the other agents of 'flu but it can be the sole cause of respiratory disease in cats.

- Disease due to *Bordetella bronchiseptica* alone usually causes mild sneezing, eye and nasal discharge, and occasionally coughing, although it has been isolated from some cases of pneumonia in kittens. It is thought occasionally to affect people.
- Treatment with antibiotics can help reduce the severity of signs and in severe cases supportive therapy is very important.
- The vaccine is administered nasally rather than by injection.

Feline leukaemia
- This disease, caused by feline leukaemia virus (FeLV), is devastating to cats. It damages the cat's immune system and can cause cancer, most commonly lymphoma.
- Cats that do not go outside and live in a FeLV-free household are at minimal risk of contracting FeLV.
- Although the prevalence of FeLV overall in the UK is

estimated to be around one per cent, it is important that we continue to vaccinate cats against it and blood test those that are at risk of having the disease to avoid a resurgence of the disease within the cat population.

Rabies
- Rabies, an invariably fatal disease, is caused by a virus and can infect all mammals, including people. The virus is found in saliva, so rabies is usually transmitted via a bite from an infected animal. Fortunately, the UK is considered rabies-free, so vaccination against this disease is not routine.
- However, a rabies vaccination is required for cats travelling abroad and returning to the UK (under the PETS travel scheme), cats being exported to a country that requires rabies vaccination, and cats entering quarantine.
- For more information on the PETS travel scheme and taking your cat abroad,

Many kittens suffer from roundworms, so routine worming is essential.
Photo: Betty Chadwick

consult the DEFRA website or your local vet. You must investigate these options well before travelling, as vaccinations and paperwork need to be started up to eight months in advance.

PARASITE CONTROL

Cats are susceptible to many different parasites. The most common and most significant ones are: roundworm, tapeworm, and fleas.

ROUNDWORMS

There are two types of roundworms that cats can have: *Toxocara cati* and *Toxocara leonina*. The eggs of both of these can be passed to other cats, rodents and, rarely, people by ingesting faeces that have eggs in them. So, cats can get roundworms by eating rodents that have eaten eggs or by ingesting faeces that have eggs in them.

Larvae of *Toxocara cati* are

commonly passed to kittens in the mother's milk. Heavy infestations will cause a failure to thrive, poor coat, diarrhoea and a pot-bellied appearance, so it is very important to treat kittens for roundworm every two weeks, from six weeks until four months of age.

In adult cats, it may not be easy to detect roundworm infestation. Occasionally, worms will be seen in vomit or faeces. How often an adult cat needs treatment for roundworm will vary depending on its lifestyle, but the general recommendation is every three to six months.

Although extremely rare, it is important to be aware that people, usually children, can become ill after ingesting infective roundworm eggs. The larval form travels through the body and may cause a disease called visceral larval migrans; it can cause eye damage and blindness. In addition to regular preventive treatment for roundworm, it is important to ensure children don't handle

faeces, don't put dirty fingers in their mouths, and wash their hands regularly.

There are many different formulations available for treating roundworms – tablets, liquid, paste, granules and spot-on – and many products will treat both roundworms and tapeworms. Consult your vet as to the product type, formulation and frequency of treatment that is most appropriate for your cat.

Most rescue centres treat their cats for roundworms, so it is wise to ask what treatment they've had and when the next one is due.

TAPEWORMS

The most common tapeworms found in cats are *Dipylidium caninum* and *Taenia taeniaformis*. A cat becomes infected with the larvae of *Dipylidium caninum* when it ingests a flea (usually during grooming) that has ingested the tapeworm eggs. This is one reason why it is so important to treat your cat regularly for fleas.

Taenia taeniaformis is contracted when cats hunt and eat rodents that have ingested parasite eggs. Tapeworms are mainly seen in older cats. However, a kitten that is infected with fleas could be infected with *Dipylidium caninum*. In fact, any cat that has fleas will be at risk of *Dipylidium* infestation.

As with roundworm, heavy infestations of tapeworm will cause health problems. Tapeworm is identified by finding segments of the worm (which are full of eggs) that look like grains of rice in the cat's faeces or areas where the cat lies.

Again, treatment for tapeworms will usually have been given to a rescue cat, but it is best to ask. Consult your vet about which product is suitable and how often to treat, because this will depend on whether the cat hunts actively and whether he is regularly treated for fleas.

Tapeworm can affect the cat that hunts and eats its prey.

Photo: Betty Chadwick

FLEAS

Fleas are a very common parasite of both cats and dogs, especially the cat flea *Ctenocephalides felis*. Cats can also be infected with rabbit or hedgehog fleas. Often it is difficult to tell if a cat is

If fleas are left untreated, your cat may well develop a skin allergy (see inset).

Photos: Cats Protection

infected with fleas, but it is important to control them because many cats are sensitive to flea saliva and will develop a traumatic skin disease called flea allergy dermatitis (FAD). Also, since fleas can carry tapeworm larvae, controlling them will also help control tapeworm infestation. Kittens with a heavy flea burden can become anaemic and weak because fleas feed on a cat's blood. Also, fleas may bite people! As you can see, regular treatment goes a long way to help prevent disease and discomfort.

The adult flea lays eggs that

develop into larvae. Eggs and larvae are found mainly in the environment, such as the cat's bed, favourite sleeping places, or carpet. Larvae particularly like dark, low traffic areas, such as carpet under beds and dressers.

The larvae develop into pupae in a cocoon, which eventually hatch into fleas, and the cycle continues. The time required for a complete cycle is variable and depends on the environment – in warm environments it can be as short as 14 days. If conditions aren't favourable for hatching, the pupae can lie dormant for up to two years.

You must treat both the cat and the environment to tackle all stages of the life cycle. Some products that are available for dogs are toxic to cats, so it is very important to consult your vet before treatment.

Rescue cats will be treated for fleas, and centres use regular environmental treatment to reduce the likelihood of infection.

DISEASES AND CONDITIONS

This list is by no means exhaustive and the descriptions are not comprehensive. They are meant to provide an introduction to the topic to help inform you of what you might experience with your cat. Your vet or other suitable medical resource will be able to provide more detail.

Feline leukaemia virus (FeLV)

This virus is present in an infected cat's saliva, so the disease can be spread via mutual grooming, sharing food and water bowls, and other forms of close contact, such as mating and fighting. There is no cure for this disease and life expectancy is reduced.

There is a test for this disease that looks for the presence of the virus in the cat's blood. It can take 30 days after being infected before the virus is detectable. Many rescue centres will blood test a cat if his history suggests that he is at

risk of having the disease and especially if the cat is showing signs of FeLV infection.

As FeLV is infectious to other cats, it is recommended that FeLV-infected cats are kept indoors or have access to controlled outdoor areas.

FeLV is also discussed briefly in the section on vaccination – see page 128.

Feline immunodeficiency virus (FIV)

This virus infects only cats and is transmitted mainly through bite wounds. Once thought to be a deadly disease in *all* cats infected, it is now known that some cats can live a long, mainly healthy life after being infected with the virus. Because signs may not appear until long after infection, illness is seen more commonly in middle-aged and older cats. Cats that do eventually show the effects of the virus will have a poorly functioning immune system and will be vulnerable to a variety of persistent or recurrent problems, such as inflamed gums, skin infections, chest infections, gut problems and weight loss.

Cats infected with FIV, even if they appear healthy, can pass the virus on to other cats. To reduce the spread of the disease, it is recommended that FIV-infected cats are kept indoors or have access to controlled outdoor areas, such as a large pen, where they will not come in close contact with other cats. The prevalence of FIV infection in the healthy cat population is thought to be around five per cent. Unneutered male cats, those that fight and those that are free-living (e.g. feral) are more at risk of contracting the disease.

There is currently no vaccine for FIV in the UK. Like FeLV, there is a blood test, which looks for antibodies to the virus. It can be up to 60 days after being exposed to the virus before a cat will test positive for FIV antibodies. Because the clinical signs of FIV and FeLV are similar, cats are often blood tested for both diseases at the same time.

Dental disease

Of the several diseases of the teeth and gums, the one that affects nearly all cats at some time in their lives is build-up of bacterial plaque on the teeth near the gums. When mineralised, this is called calculus or tartar. If the calculus builds up over time, it can cause inflammation of the gums (gingivitis), leading to infection in the gums, around the tooth and root (peridontitis) and possibly even the root itself, so regular dental care is important to help prevent this (see Chapter Four, page 98). Often the hard calculus needs to be

Preventative health care, such as teeth-brushing and providing a suitable diet, will help to combat dental disease.
Photo: Betty Chadwick

removed by a process called scaling, which is done under general anaesthetic. The earlier this is done, the longer we can keep the teeth and gums healthy.

Juvenile gingivitis is an inflammation of the gums in kittens between the ages of three and seven months. The cause is not known, but it usually clears up spontaneously.

The most significant and cat-specific dental disease is Feline Odontoclastic Resorptive Lesions (FORL). These relatively common erosive lesions occur at the junction of the crown and root of the tooth.

They are sometimes visible above the gum line but more often are located below the gum line and are thus not easily seen.

The cause of FORL is not known. Treatment is to remove the affected teeth. The erosion of the tooth causes it to weaken, and it may break off spontaneously or when the tooth is being extracted.

Digestive problems

The main signs of a problem with the digestive tract are vomiting, diarrhoea and constipation. For each of these signs, there are many possible causes. Primary digestive disorders originate in the digestive tract itself, while secondary disorders result from a disease process elsewhere in the body.

Examples of primary causes of gastrointestinal disease are: infection (bacteria, viruses, parasites), diet, ingestion of toxins, physical obstruction or narrowing of the gastrointestinal tract (e.g. foreign body, tumour, strictures, cancer), damage to the nerve supply of the intestines, and non-specific inflammation of the intestinal tissue.

Examples of secondary causes of gastrointestinal disease are: narrowing of the pelvic canal after damage to the pelvis (usually after a road traffic accident), hyperthyroidism, liver disease, kidney disease, stress, unwillingness to use the

In most cases, a cat with hair-ball problems will vomit up a ball after grooming.

Photo: Mary Drown

litter tray, exocrine pancreatic insufficiency (EPI), which can result after damage to the pancreas, infection with FeLV or FIV.

If a cat shows any signs of a digestive problem, or is not eating or drinking, it is important that he is examined by a vet to try to determine the cause, to ensure that the cat does not become dehydrated, and to try to get the cat eating again.

Because cats are fastidious groomers, they ingest a lot of hair. In some cats, particularly but not exclusively long-haired cats, this can create balls of hair that are difficult to digest and pass through the digestive system. Usually the hair-ball is vomited up, and, if we're lucky, we see this and can diagnose the problem. If a cat does have a problem with hair-balls, specially formulated foods or pastes are available that will help the hair-balls pass through the intestinal tract.

Feline lower urinary tract disease (FLUTD)

FLUTD is a term that encompasses all the conditions that can cause problems with the bladder and passage of urine in the cat. There are many causes of urinary tract disease but in cats most cases are idiopathic, that is, the cause isn't known. When this is the case, the disease is called Feline Idiopathic Cystitis or FIC.

It is important to know the signs of FLUTD, because veterinary attention will be required. Common signs are difficulty or inability (this is more serious) to pass urine, pain when urinating, sometimes aggressive behaviour, urinating outside the litter tray, blood in the urine, and urinating more often than usual.

Stress is known to contribute to flare-ups of FIC, so in a cat susceptible to this disease, minimising stress is a key part of managing this condition.

If your cat shows any of the above signs, it is important to seek veterinary advice.

OWNER'S HEALTH CONCERNS

Some people worry about the diseases they might catch from a cat. The chances of this happening are very low; in fact, you're more likely to catch something from another human than from your cat! However, some people are more susceptible than others so the elderly, pregnant women, those receiving chemotherapy treatment and people with compromised immune systems may be interested in the following two commonly talked about conditions.

Ringworm

Ringworm is an infection caused by a fungus that grows in the dead, surface layers of the hair or claws. It has nothing to do with worms. The appearance of cats with ringworm is very variable. Some cats show skin lesions, hair loss and scaling skin whilst others can appear completely normal showing no skin lesions or hair loss. Long-haired cats

A longhaired cat is more likely to be affected with ringworm.
Photo: Sue Cooper

are often particularly badly affected. Treatment consists of three essential elements:
• Anti-fungal drugs administered by mouth.
• Shampooing your cat's fur.
• Decontaminating the environment.

Ringworm can also be spread to humans (seen in the form of small patches of thickened reddened skin or patches of hair loss) so direct contact with an infected cat should be minimised. When treating a cat wear rubber gloves and protective clothing. Most cases of human ringworm are treated with a fungicidal cream.

Toxoplasmosis

Toxoplasma is a tiny parasite that lives within cells in the body. Cats are infected by eating diseased prey or raw meat. Stray cats and those that hunt a lot are most likely to be infected.

A cat may show no sign of infection but can show vague illness (tiredness, weight loss and a high temperature) if their immune system is not working well. Most cats once infected will become immune and will shed infective particles(oocysts) in their faeces for a short time only. Oocysts only become infective 24 hours after exposure to the air.

There is very little risk to people of contracting toxoplasmosis from their cat. The most common way for people to get toxoplasmosis is by ingestion of the oocysts from contaminated fruit and vegetables and inadequately cooked meat. However those at greater risk should not empty the cat litter tray and should wear gloves when gardening. The litter tray should be cleaned using boiling water.

SUMMARY

Rescue cats come from all sorts of backgrounds: from a home where an elderly person has passed away, from a family household with lots of people, from a household with lots of cats or other animals, or from having lost their way and living 'rough'. This means that their health status can be quite variable – from tip-top

Rescued cats come in all shapes and sizes and from a variety of backgrounds.

Photo: Tony Willitt

A cat is an amazing animal to share your life with, and you will be amply rewarded for the care that you give.
Photo: Martin Dawe photography

condition to having a recognised, ongoing problem, such as FIV infection.

As a cat owner, you can do much to maintain the health of your beloved pet and to prevent disease. The key elements of health maintenance and disease prevention for your cat are:

- Provide a balanced, good-quality diet
- Recognise and look after his behavioural needs
- Do home dental care
- Groom his coat
- Have him neutered
- Vaccinate regularly
- Treat for parasites regularly
- Visit the vet for regular health checks.

Above all, be enriched by the special bond that is formed through our relationship with our feline friends.

ABOUT CATS PROTECTION

Cats Protection is the UK's leading feline welfare charity. Established since 1927, we rescue and rehome around 60,000 cats and kittens every year through our nationwide network of 29 Adoption Centres and 260 voluntary-run Branches.

We receive no government funding, so rely entirely on public generosity to finance our vital work. There are many ways in which you can help us.

- Adopt a rescue cat or kitten
- Make a donation
- Leave a legacy/bequest
- Become a volunteer
- Sponsor a cat cabin

If you are looking for a companion to share your life with, we have many gorgeous cats in our care awaiting loving, caring homes.

To find your nearest Cats Protection Adoption Centre or Branch, or for further information, please phone our Helpline on 08702 099 099 (open Mon–Fri 9–5pm), visit our website at www.cats.org.uk or write to us at Cats Protection, National Cat Centre, Chelwood Gate, Haywards Heath, Sussex. RH17 7TT.

Whatever you do, you'll be making a big difference to the cats in our care.

WHERE YOU CAN FIND US

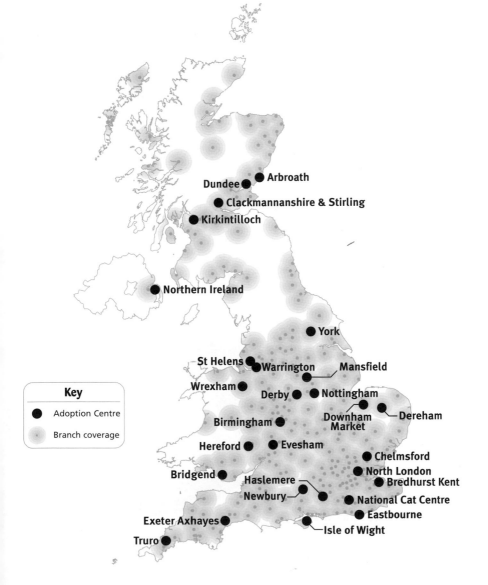

Shetland

Arbroath
Dundee
Clackmannanshire & Stirling
Kirkintilloch

Northern Ireland

York

St Helens
Warrington
Wrexham
Derby
Nottingham
Mansfield
Downham Market
Dereham
Birmingham
Hereford
Evesham
Chelmsford
North London
Bredhurst Kent
Bridgend
Haslemere
Newbury
National Cat Centre
Exeter Axhayes
Eastbourne
Isle of Wight
Truro

Key
● Adoption Centre
⬤ Branch coverage

HAPPY ENDINGS

Giving cats a second chance is what we're all about! Here are just a few of our success stories.

TINY TIGER

Tiger was just a week old when he came into the care of the South Birmingham Branch. Fosterer, Mary Berry, had to feed him every two hours – day and night – to ensure this tiny kitten survived. Thanks to Mary's efforts Tiger did make it and is now enjoying a very active life with his new owners!

After a shaky start, Tiger is now living up to his name with his new owners.
Photo: Cats Protection

A GOOD SPIRIT

Life was looking bleak for stray cat, Brooke, when he came into the care of our Kirkintilloch Adoption Centre near Glasgow. Fortunately though, he got lucky when the Famous Grouse Distillery chose him to be their 'meet and greet cat'. Brooke now welcomes 120,000 visitors a year into the distillery and gets thoroughly spoilt by the staff. A real 'from rags to riches' tale!

Brooke – from rags to riches!
Photo: Alan Richardson